THE ONLY THING

A STUDY IN SPIRITUALITY

THAT COUNTS

VIC DELAMONT

WESTBOW
PRESS®
A DIVISION OF THOMAS NELSON
& ZONDERVAN

WestBow Press books may be ordered through booksellers or by contacting:

WestBow Press
A Division of Thomas Nelson & Zondervan
1663 Liberty Drive
Bloomington, IN 47403
www.westbowpress.com
1 (866) 928-1240

ISBN: 978-1-9736-3547-5 (sc)
ISBN: 978-1-9736-3548-2 (hc)
ISBN: 978-1-9736-3546-8 (e)

Library of Congress Control Number: 2018908914

Print information available on the last page.

WestBow Press rev. date: 9/17/2018

CONTENTS

PREFACE AND ACKNOWLEDGEMENTS

This book is different from anything else you have read. It fearlessly addresses issues that others seem afraid to ask about: Is spirituality personal or absolute? Does it really matter what I think? Does spirituality have anything to do with the "big" questions in life – my worldview, how I make my choices, the will of God (whatever that is...)?

As I have sought to guide my readers into finding answers to these potentially life-changing questions, I owe a debt of thanks to many people for their efforts in helping me release this manuscript. Some of those people include:

Bev Delamont – my beloved wife, for her editing, proof reading and patience as I worked on this manuscript for so many years.

My friends in the small group Bible study that I have had the privilege of leading in recent years, who went through the material with me as a study, and tore it apart quite mercifully: David and Gwen Hall, Chuck and Lynda Hess, Wayne and Royaleen Hewitt, Gary and Donna Jackson, Andy and Sue Little, Rick and Deirdre Merryfield.

Author, Suzanne Benner, for her critical reading and very helpful suggestions.

Finally, to my editorial, design and marketing colleagues at Westbow Press for their invaluable assistance in getting this book to print.

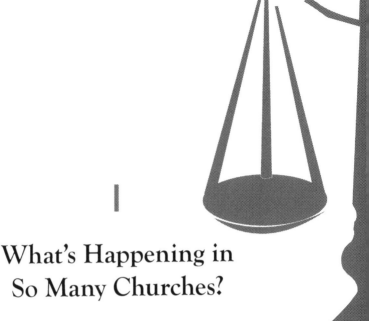

What's Happening in So Many Churches?

Michael and Jen were struggling. It seemed to them that a relationship with God had to have more significance than they felt theirs did. It didn't seem like most of the people worshipping in their church were genuine; why? Even right after the service, nobody seemed to actually talk about spiritual things as much as they did about the game, their jobs, or *anything* else. And they became really uncomfortable when those two board members discussed that new staff member's performance with them. They were a fairly new couple in the church, and in their faith, and just didn't know how to respond. Then Chris's reaction at work today; well, it was just devastating to them both.

You see, Michael had tried to tell Chris about his new faith in Jesus. His business partner's caustic accusations about some of the people in Michael's church caught him off guard. According to Chris, they said one thing but lived another. In his opinion, their claims of a "new life in Christ" just didn't seem valid. These so-called Christians were always late paying their outstanding accounts to the company he and Michael ran. And one of their employees, who was also a member of Michael's church, was well known for wanting to hear off-color stories the guys in the shop told, but he had such a holier-than-thou attitude at other times. Michael couldn't answer him. He didn't know what to say.

Michael discussed this really uncomfortable conversation with Jen; they thought deeply about Chris's harsh response. What distressed them most was that what he had said, actually seemed to be accurate. Maybe they were in the wrong congregation, but they had been welcomed so warmly there. The pastor had involved them in a growth class right away, and they had really grown in their faith. They truly wondered what to do.

Does this story sound familiar to you? Could it be told in a church you know? The intent of this book is to examine how we might move beyond some very real limitations in the way many average Christians seem to live, learn to understand what biblical spirituality is, and then look at how (if it is at all possible) we can actually move into it.

To begin with (just as an enlightening exercise), stop reading at the end of this sentence and list, in your own mind, the truly biblically spiritual people you know. Now, is your list distressingly short? Most are. The shortness of that list may be an indication of the weakened state of the church in North America (where most of my readers reside) at this point in the twenty-first century. Where is the *reality* of spirituality? Michael and Jen were coming to grips with a basic, tragic question. Sure, everybody talks about being spiritual right now. It's culturally acceptable to be spiritual. But why is it so unacceptable to be *biblical*, or even Christian? Those who have been believers for much longer than Michael and Jen also struggle with the same issue; why are there so few seemingly genuinely biblically spiritual people around? You know the kind, the spiritual giants we wish we could be like, the ones who move us to maybe wonder why we aren't like them, or to question why we don't have the same vital relationship with God they do (or they seem to). Can you count on one hand the number that you've met, maybe even in a lifetime? Why aren't all believers like them? Instead, there seem to be so few, so regrettably, very few.

This lack of biblical spirituality among us contributes to many things. Bible-believing churches may be growing, but there seems to be fewer individual believers leading others to Christ. Perhaps a good deal of our church growth is transfer growth from other congregations that are dwindling or from rural areas to towns and cities. There may be many people attending church, but finding qualified workers to maintain (never mind expand) the programs is increasingly difficult. Mission boards are actively recruiting new missionaries (albeit with different roles than traditional ones had), while those recruited years before are returning home, for lack of adequate funds for their personal and ministry needs. Our seminaries are turning out a fairly significant number of graduates, but most of them will stay at home, not having received the call to minister in an evangelism setting or a discipleship function. Many end up in maintenance roles. Finally (for now), and perhaps the most distressing perception of all, is that it appears that true biblical spirituality is accepted as being out of reach for the average Christian. We are becoming reconciled to the thought that "so-so" is the reality we have to live with (even though it sure feels good to be able to sing the worship songs about how great it is to be a believer).

So what's the problem?

Four degrees and nearly three decades of involvement in ministry and communications in Canadian and US churches, missions, and media outlets doesn't qualify me to write about this vital issue, but it *has* given me a valuable perspective based on contact with many other leaders and believers. I actually feel called to address this problem. I believe in the vital significance of this subject. I believe that I *must* address it, but not because I feel worthy. After years of prayer, preparation, and study and a sincere desire to honor God in my own life, I firmly believe that this apparent lack of true spirituality is the central issue facing the church today. I also believe that the solution to this central issue can be summarized by one word: *attitude*.

While I propose this simple, one-word answer to a wide array of problems, the solution itself is by no means simplistic. Any proposed antidote for a malady as serious as a lack of biblical spirituality must be broad enough to address the many difficulties that we encounter as Christians. The missing ingredient of true biblical spirituality may well be the most serious factor we will ever consider in our desire to live as believers who are true followers of Jesus Christ. On the basis of our perception of what true spirituality is, whether it's realistic and whether we want it or not, our lives will rise or fall in both significance and enjoyment.

Here's where I'm coming from, my perspective and presuppositions:

- I am assuming that I am addressing Bible-believing people, who are facing the current cultural and global challenges of the twenty-first century. (If you are not yet of this Bible-believing persuasion, the remainder of this book will explain why you should be.)
- Further, that you are somewhat (if not greatly) distressed at a lack of spiritual vitality and reality either in your own life or in that of others in your group.
- You believe that what God's Word has to say about the subject is more important and instructive than anything I could say (so I will rely heavily on quotations and applications from Scripture).
- You want to believe there must be more to true faith than what we so often settle for.

We are all spiritual beings, because the Creator God made us to be so. Since the one who made us to be spiritual beings has revealed how we should live in a manual, called the Bible, it seems only logical that we should look to that instruction book to determine how best to live successfully in the world He designed for us. It would be foolish to ignore the manufacturer's instruction manual, so I'll rely heavily on Scripture for both authoritative guidance and hopeful insights.

This chapter speaks to this final point two paragraphs above (there must be more to true faith), for only after we've been convinced that true biblical spirituality is indeed possible will we be willing to pursue it with any kind of conviction. We don't need or want another quick fix. What we *do* desperately need is a vibrant, lasting relationship with the one true and living God of the Bible. My thesis is that biblical spirituality is only possible with this relationship.

ATTITUDES

In order to tackle this core topic productively, we must have a clear understanding of what the Bible has to say to us about our attitudes. As an opening thought as to the importance of our mindset, consider the following reference. It attests to the value of a proper attitude that truly seeks to know God. This Old Testament example is taken from the instructions David gave to his son, Solomon:

> And you, my son Solomon, acknowledge the God
> of your father, and serve him with wholehearted
> devotion and with a *willing mind*, for the LORD
> searches every *heart* and understands every
> *motive* behind the *thoughts*. If you seek him, he
> will be found by you; but if you forsake him, he
> will reject you forever. (1 Chronicles 28:9)

Look at the modifiers: "wholehearted devotion," "willing mind." Examine the words that indicate Solomon's involvement (or ours): "willing mind," "every heart," "every motive," "seek him," "forsake him." Are these typical of our involvement with God today? In what ways might our attitude toward God be revealed? That's what we're going to discover together. As you will find out, attitude is central to the remainder of this book.

2

The Foundation of
Biblical Spirituality

Michael and Jen decided to go and talk to their pastor about their struggles. As their story unfolded, tears came to the pastor's eyes. He then did something that was rare for a minister to do: He shared his frustrations with them. Their pastor had felt a call of God to go into ministry to "build up the body in the most holy faith," as he put it. But, by his own estimation, that wasn't happening. Many of the people in his congregation didn't seem to be growing more like Christ at all. Oh sure, there were a few encouraging signs here and there. (The pastor likened it to a poor golfer getting just enough good shots to keep him coming back to play another round.) He told them that he had even been thinking of quitting the ministry. He was becoming convinced that the lack of noticeable growth in his congregation was all his fault.

As they talked together, they realized that the observations Michael's partner, Chris, had made were indeed accurate, but maybe not unavoidable. Their pastor had been trying to teach these truths to his people, and Michael and Jen had been trying to live them, but it felt like so few others seemed either able or willing to sustain spiritual development. Why was it such a pervasive problem in the church? Their pastor actually had the answer. He had been trying to pray it, preach it and teach it for years. Though his message seemed largely unheeded, it was accurate: "The only thing that counts is faith expressing itself through love." It's not what you do; it's *why and how* you do it.

Does that sound way too simple for you? Then what's the foundational principle for your living a biblically spiritual life? Is your system working to lead you closer to Jesus and make your life more like His? If so, I truly thank God for you and your belief system, whatever it may be. While our opinions may vary somewhat, I believe that the Bible gives us this definite summary for our instruction:

THE ONLY THING THAT COUNTS IS FAITH
EXPRESSING ITSELF THROUGH LOVE.

This synopsis is given to us by the apostle Paul, in Galatians 5:6. Here is the context of the thought, taken from Galatians 5:4 through 6:10. Notice, once again, the motivations and attitudes referred to in this passage:

> You who are trying to be justified by law have been alienated from Christ; you have fallen away from grace. But by faith we eagerly await through the Spirit the righteousness for which we hope. For *in Christ Jesus* [italics indicate emphasis added, here and throughout the book] neither circumcision nor uncircumcision has any value. The only thing that counts is faith expressing itself through love.
>
> You were running a good race. Who cut in on you and kept you from obeying the truth? That

kind of persuasion does not come from the one who calls you. "A little yeast works through the whole batch of dough." I am confident in the Lord that you will take no other view. The one who is throwing you into confusion will pay the penalty, whoever he may be. Brothers, if I am still preaching circumcision, why am I still being persecuted? In that case the offense of the cross has been abolished. As for those agitators, I wish they would go the whole way and emasculate themselves!

You, my brothers, were called to be free. But do not use your freedom to indulge the sinful nature, rather, serve one another in love. The entire law is summed up in a single command: *"Love your neighbor as yourself."* If you keep on biting and devouring each other, watch out or you will be destroyed by each other.

So I say, *live by the Spirit,* and you will not gratify the desires of the sinful nature. For the sinful nature desires what is contrary to the Spirit, and the Spirit what is contrary to the sinful nature. They are in conflict with each other, so that you do not do what you want. But if you are led by the Spirit, you are not under law. The acts of the sinful nature are obvious: sexual immorality, impurity and debauchery; idolatry and witchcraft; hatred, discord, jealousy, fits of rage, selfish ambition, dissensions, factions and envy; drunkenness, orgies, and the like. I warn you, as I did before, that those who live like this will not inherit the kingdom of God.

But the fruit of the Spirit is *love, joy, peace, patience, kindness, goodness, faithfulness, gentleness and self-control.* Against such things there is no law. Those who belong to Christ Jesus have crucified the sinful nature with its passions and desires. Since we live by the Spirit, let us keep in step with the Spirit. Let us not become conceited, provoking and envying each other.

Brothers, if someone is caught in a sin, you who are spiritual should restore him gently. But watch yourself, or you also may be tempted. Carry each other's burdens, and in this way you will fulfill the law of Christ. If anyone thinks he is something when he is nothing, he deceives himself. Each one should test his own actions. Then he can take pride in himself, without comparing himself to somebody else, for each one should carry his own load.

Anyone who receives instruction in the word must share all good things with his instructor. Do not be deceived: God cannot be mocked. A man reaps what he sows. The one who sows to please his sinful nature, from that nature will reap destruction; the one who sows to please the Spirit, from the Spirit will reap eternal life. Let us not become weary in doing good, for at the proper time we will reap a harvest if we do not give up. Therefore, as we have opportunity, let us do good to all people, especially to those who belong to the family of believers.

(We will return to the concept of doing in chapter 11.)

A discussion of Paul's context is fitting, I believe, to the subject of this book, as well. He is addressing those who felt a need to abide by all the rules, to *do* what ought to be done. This treatise of Paul's falls right on the heels of his words from the end of chapter 2 and the beginning of chapter 3. Here is the argument he is presenting. Bear in mind, though, that the prelude to it *all* contextually, is those who are "in Christ Jesus," those in the church.

> We who are Jews by birth and not "Gentile sinners" know that *a man is not justified by observing the law, but by faith in Jesus Christ.* So we, too, have put our faith in Christ Jesus that we may be justified by faith in Christ and not by observing the law, because by observing the law no one will be justified. If, while we seek to be justified in Christ, it becomes evident that we ourselves are sinners, does that mean that Christ promotes sin? Absolutely not! If I rebuild what I destroyed, I prove that I am a lawbreaker. For through the law I died to the law so that I might live for God. I have been crucified with Christ and I no longer live, but *Christ lives in me.* The life I live in the body, I live by faith in the Son of God, who loved me and gave himself for me. I do not set aside the grace of God, for if righteousness could be gained through the law, Christ died for nothing!

> You foolish Galatians! Who has bewitched you? Before your very eyes Jesus Christ was clearly portrayed as crucified. I would like to learn just one thing from you: Did you receive the Spirit by observing the law, or by believing what you

heard? Are you so foolish? After beginning with the Spirit, are you now trying to attain your goal by human effort? Have you suffered so much for nothing—if it really was for nothing? Does God give you his Spirit and work miracles among you because you observe the law, or because you believe what you heard?

Consider Abraham: "He believed God, and it was credited to him as righteousness." Understand, then, that those who believe are children of Abraham. The scripture foresaw that God would justify the Gentiles by faith, and announced the gospel in advance to Abraham: "All nations will be blessed through you." So those who have faith are blessed along with Abraham, the man of faith.

All who rely on observing the law are under a curse, for it is written: "Cursed is everyone who does not continue to do everything written in the Book of the Law." Clearly no one is justified before God by the law, because, "The righteous will live by faith." (Galatians 2:15–3:11)

The problems addressed here are so similar to those of Michael and Jen's church, my church, and probably yours too. (Don't you find that sometimes one can only marvel at how little we humans seem to have really advanced over the years?) Well, ours is surely not the first generation to struggle with trying to balance being a believer with living in the world without adopting its values and practices. But we, as Christians in any generation, have the blessed assurance that God is not taken by surprise. And more than that, He has both anticipated our dilemma and graciously provided instruction for us that will guide us through this struggle.

If it is really true that the essence of the whole matter, or as Paul puts it, "the only thing that counts," is our underlying attitude, our faith, expressing itself in love (and I've no reason to doubt this), then what specifically *are* the attitudes, motivations, and responses that God expects of us, based on this declaration? For this, again, we turn to our only authoritative guide for faith and practice: the Bible. Consider the weight and significance of the following selections. They will deal with two fundamental concepts: We are holy travelers who are in a real battle, who therefore must make a conscious decision as to how we will live, and who have the example of Christ and the encouragement of Scripture to guide us. By the way, things that *don't* matter include the group we came from (our religious history) and our present religious status.

The first Scripture passage we will consider is found in 1 Peter 1:13–2:3.

WE ARE HOLY TRAVELERS

> Therefore, prepare your minds for action; be self-controlled; set your hope fully on the grace to be given you when Jesus Christ is revealed. As obedient children, do not conform to the evil desires you had when you lived in ignorance. But just as he who called you is holy, so be holy in all you do; for it is written: "Be holy, because I am holy."
>
> Since you call on a Father who judges each man's work impartially, live your lives as strangers here in reverent fear. For you know that it was not with perishable things such as silver or gold that you were redeemed from the empty way of

life handed down to you from your forefathers, but with the precious blood of Christ, a lamb without blemish or defect. He was chosen before the creation of the world, but was revealed in these last times for your sake. *Through him you believe in God*, who raised him from the dead and glorified him, and so your *faith and hope* are in God.

Now that you have purified yourselves by obeying the truth so that you have sincere love for your brothers, love one another deeply, *from the heart*. For you have been born again, not of perishable seed, but of imperishable, through the living and enduring word of God. For, "All men are like grass, and all their glory is like the flowers of the field; the grass withers and the flowers fall, but the word of the Lord stands forever." And this is the word that was preached to you.

Therefore, rid yourselves of all malice and all deceit, hypocrisy, envy, and slander of every kind. Like newborn babies, crave pure spiritual milk, so that by it you may grow up in your salvation, now that you have tasted that the Lord is good.

In review:

- Get your mind in gear.
- Do not conform to your evil desires.
- Judgment is coming.
- Recognize that God cares for you.
- Purify yourself by obedience to love.

It's difficult, isn't it, to live in this world and not be a part of it or be stained by it? (You may wish to review John 17 here.) But God knows that. Why else would He have sent His Son to die and rise again, and then graciously give His Holy Spirit to live in those who trust Him as Savior? "I have told you these things so that in me you may have peace. In this world you will have trouble. But take heart! I have overcome the world" (John 16:33).

It's time for each of us to decide whether we truly *believe* God or whether we don't. I am convinced that if we answer this one question honestly, we'll know whether we believe Him fully or not: Would God command us to live in a way that was impossible to achieve? Can you trust Him to do in and through you what He says He can and will? If He demanded something impossible, wouldn't that be unjust (or at least harsh)? But He demands only that which is not only possible, but which He will do for you (Ephesians 4:22–24; Philippians 2:13). He is merciful, loving, and genuinely God. Can you trust Him to do through you what He says He will do? Of course, you can (this is part of the promised role of the Holy Spirit), but will you trust Him fully? What attitude will you need to adopt in order for this to become your ongoing pattern of life? Part of the purpose of this book is to help you get there.

THE BATTLE IS REAL

Many people live as though there were no spiritual battles going on at all. They don't pray for spiritual victories in the lives of friends or family, for those in ministries, for those in missions work, or for those they are attempting to be an influence on for Jesus Christ. Oh sure, there may be some sort of spiritual darkness out there that needs to be defeated, but it's in some other neighborhood or in some other part of the world. Dear God, please forgive us for our blindness and hardness. The truth is that we *are* in a battle; what kind of person stands surrounded by warfare and doesn't even acknowledge that there is a fight on, let alone at least try to protect himself and his loved ones? Listen, friend:

> For though we live in the world, we do not wage war as the world does. The weapons we fight with are not the weapons of the world. On the contrary, *they have divine power* to demolish strongholds. We demolish arguments and every pretension that sets itself up against *the knowledge of God*, and we take captive *every thought* to make it obedient to Christ. (2 Corinthians 10:3–5)

Do you want to win the battle, the battle that you were perhaps unwilling to admit was even real in your life? You can. You have the power to demolish strongholds, even those strongholds in your mind. What are our main enemies in this battle? The "arguments and ... pretension[s] that set [themselves] up against the knowledge of God." Did you previously understand that *knowing God is what the battle is all about?* The devil doesn't want you (or anyone else) to really know God; the flesh doesn't, either. All the evil forces you can imagine are attempting to persuade you that you can't *really* know Him, that there are reasonable arguments that support their claims, and that you're doing okay, anyway. These very thoughts are the enemies of your soul.

You're in a battle, all right, but it's a moment-by-moment battle that you can win. How? By "tak[ing] captive every thought to make it obedient to Christ." This has nothing to do with going to church regularly, but it has everything to do with why you make the choice to attend. It has nothing to do with the actual level of your giving, but it has everything to do with how you *choose* that level of giving. It has nothing to do with any outward function, sign, or evidence of a claim to be Christian. It has everything to do with whether you are an obedient one or not. "If you love me, you will obey what I command" (John 14:15). By the way, can you even *be* a Christian and not love Jesus? And can you love Him and not obey Him? Dear reader, do what you need to do. Take your thoughts captive through the power of the Spirit of Almighty God. Recognize that you can't do life on your own, but that He can make it real for you by His Holy Spirit working through you. How? Read on:

> Therefore, my dear friends, as you have always obeyed—not only in my presence, but now much more in my absence—continue to work out your salvation with fear and trembling. (Philippians 2:12)

Now, what does the Bible mean when it instructs us to "work out our own salvation"? Does it mean that we are responsible to work it out by ourselves, with whatever that might imply? Well, yes and no. Yes, it is our responsibility, but no, it is not our job. The very next verse points out that "it is God who works in you to will and to act according to his good purpose" (Philippians 2:13).

There's a lot in here. Let's look at it piece by piece.

First of all, we are to work out that which is within us. What's in us? God at work. Do you think He can fulfill His own wishes and commands? Of course, He can, and He is in *you*, if you have trusted Him fully, by faith, as Savior and Lord (Ephesians 2:8–9).

Second, the power "to will and to act" are both His as well. You don't desire what you should? Work out what's already within you. You don't feel you have the spiritual strength to do what you ought? Work out what's already within you. The responsibility to make the choice to live right is yours and yours alone. The power to do it is God's and God's alone. (Chapter 9 is about your worldview. There, we will discuss how none of us can fulfill even the very basic requisites for being a Christian by our own efforts, but God surely can. He has taken upon Himself *all* of the impossibilities; knowing that in ourselves, we cannot live as Christians, we will therefore rely totally and completely on Him.) Do you want more help now, in controlling your thoughts, for example?

THE ATTITUDE OF CHRIST

> Your attitude should be the same as that of Christ Jesus: Who, being in very nature God, did not consider equality with God something to be grasped, but made himself nothing, taking the very nature of a servant, being made in human likeness. And being found in appearance as a man, he humbled himself and became obedient to death—even death on a cross! Therefore God exalted him to the highest place and gave him the name that is above every name, that at the name of Jesus every knee should bow, in heaven and on earth and under the earth, and every tongue confess that Jesus Christ is Lord, to the glory of God the Father.

> Therefore, my dear friends, as you have always obeyed—not only in my presence, but now much more in my absence—continue to work out your own salvation with fear and trembling, for it is God who works in you to will and to act according to his good purpose.

> Do everything without complaining or arguing, so that you may become blameless and pure, children of God without fault in a crooked and depraved generation, in which you shine like stars in the universe as you hold out the word of life.

This passage is from Philippians 2:5–16 and is the context for the two verses discussed above. In it, we are reminded how Jesus Christ is truly God. He chose to become a servant. Your attitude should be the same. He humbled Himself. Your attitude should be the same. He became obedient. Your attitude should be the same. And what will the result be? God will work in you, enabling you to become blameless and pure so that *you* will shine like a star as you hold out the word of life. Isn't that explosive? Isn't that what you want?

THE DECISION TO BE MADE

> So I tell you this, and insist on it in the Lord, that you must no longer live as the Gentiles do, *in the futility of their thinking.* They are darkened in their understanding and separated from the life of God because of the ignorance that is in them due to the *hardening of their hearts.* Having lost all sensitivity, they have given themselves over to sensuality so as to indulge in every kind of impurity, with a continual lust for more.

> You, however, did not come to know Christ that way. Surely you heard of him and were taught in him in accordance with the truth that is in Jesus. You were taught, with regard to your former way of life, to put off your old self, which is being corrupted by its deceitful desires; to be made new *in the attitude of your minds*; and to put on the new self, created to *be like God in true righteousness and holiness.* (Ephesians 4:17–24)

What does the Bible tell us is the basis of living like a pagan? Wrong thinking. Why are their thoughts not controlled and in keeping with God's character? They have hard hearts. How do you prevent this from happening? By putting off your old self, because it is being corrupted. Is it corrupted by the outside influences of evil? Most assuredly, but it is primarily being corrupted by its own *deceitful* desires, and those who are lost don't even recognize that. What's the solution? Put on your new self, through adopting a new attitude of mind. By the way, isn't that what you really want: a new self? (Renovating the old self just doesn't seem to work, does it?) Well, it *is* possible, for this new self is characterized by a likeness to God that is marked by true righteousness and holiness. Not the righteousness that you might try to generate on your own, for "all of us have become like one who is unclean, and all *our* righteous acts are like filthy rags" (Isaiah 64:6). Yuck.

Please don't think that I am speaking of the raw power of positive thinking, for I am not. Certainly, a great deal can be accomplished in this life by the applied strength of the human mind and spirit. But righteousness can never be accomplished like that, and regeneration can never result from positive thinking. Only God can bring about our salvation, and only through faith in His provision, which He freely gives to us (see Ephesians 2:8–9). No, I am addressing the attitude and mindset of people who have already come to Christ in faith. I am speaking of living a life of obedient surrender to the control of the Spirit, not of endeavoring to achieve, by being positive, that which cannot possibly be accomplished by any human alone. Only God can live a life of righteousness and holiness, and no amount of human determination will ever reach that goal without God doing it. He has chosen to accomplish this by living His life through the life of a surrendered believer.

SOME FURTHER HELP

> Finally, brothers, whatever is true, whatever is noble, whatever is right, whatever is pure, whatever is lovely, whatever is admirable—if anything is excellent or praiseworthy—think about such things. (Philippians 4:8)

Focus on the good. God is good. Push into Him. Make your relationship and your growth in your knowledge and experience of

Christ *intentional*. Every good and perfect gift is from Him. Don't deceive yourself. Rely on Him to enable you to become what you want to be (see also Ephesians 4:7–8; Psalm 34:7–10; James 1:16–17.) From 1 Corinthians 3:16–4:2, we learn about stewardship:

> Don't you know that you yourselves are God's temple and that God's Spirit lives in you? If anyone destroys God's temple, God will destroy him; for God's temple is sacred, and you are that temple. Do not deceive yourselves. If any one of you thinks he is wise by the standards of this age, he should become a "fool" so that he may become wise. For the wisdom of this world is foolishness in God's sight. As it is written: "He catches the wise in their craftiness"; and again, "The Lord knows that the thoughts of the wise are futile." So then, no more boasting about men! All things are yours [including true biblical spirituality], whether Paul or Apollos or Cephas or the world or life or death or the present or the future—all are yours, and you are of Christ, and Christ is of God. So then, men ought to regard us as servants of Christ and as those entrusted with the secret things of God. Now it is required that those who have been given a trust must prove faithful.

How is the faithfulness of a steward verified? Obedience is demonstrated by faithfully expressing itself in love. Choose to be that Christian who lives by the power of the Holy Spirit of Christ Jesus, who indwells the true believer, the one who has been born again into the family of God through living faith in Jesus's sacrifice. We have become *His* temple. You have been entrusted with the secret things of God. How remarkable is that?

3

The Prayer Life of a Christian

Our true attitude or motive often comes out in our praying. Read and contemplate this portion of the New Testament (Paul is offering a prayer on behalf of his "spiritual children" in Ephesians 3:14–21):

> For this reason I kneel before the Father, from whom his whole family in heaven and on earth derives its name. I pray that out of his glorious riches he may strengthen you with power through his Spirit in your *inner being*, so that Christ may dwell in your *hearts* through faith. And I pray that you, being rooted and established in love, may have power, together with all the saints, to grasp how wide and long and high and deep is the love of Christ, and to know this love that surpasses knowledge—that you may be filled to the measure of all the fullness of God. Now to him who is able to do immeasurably more than all we ask or imagine, according to his power that is at work within us, to him be glory in

the church and in Christ Jesus throughout all
generations, for ever and ever! Amen.

Notice what Paul prays for, in contrast with a typical prayer
offered in most of our homes or churches. We pray for health, safety,
jobs, and healing for our ill family members or friends, and we ask
God to bless us. Paul prays for strength in their inner beings, so
that Christ may dwell in their hearts and that they may be rooted
and established in love, even to the depth of understanding the
love of Christ. He further asks that these believers will know that
which surpasses knowledge, to the end that they may be filled to the
measure of all the fullness of God. Is this even possible? Humanly, of
course, it isn't. But Jesus did say, in Matthew 19:26, "With man this
is impossible, but with God all things are possible" (see also Mark
10:27, Luke 1:37 and Luke 18:27).

Why don't we pray about authentic spiritual issues more
regularly? One reason is that we are conditioned by our society
to believe that we can do anything or be anything if we try hard
enough. This is part of the so-called work ethic. This belief is the
driving force that once made the craftsmanship of Europe and then
North America the leading standard for the rest of the world. But it
may also be one of the greatest enemies of Christianity active in our
churches today, outside of the devastation wrought by Satan himself.

I'm not trying to be dramatic when I ask whether the loss of
this work ethic could, in fact, be one of the devil's tools to weaken
Christians in our day. (Thankfully, I don't know Satan's mind.) What
I do know is that the good is often the enemy of the best. We have
seemingly bought into the concept of *doing* good, Christian things but
are bottoming out in the whole area of *being* good, Christian people.

Literally stop for a moment here and think about your own prayer
life. Do you pray to be blessed, without any serious thought of how
you will pass that blessing along? Do you pray for health, but rarely
think at all about why God leaves you here on the face of the earth at
all, whether in good health or poor? Do you pray, as we were warned

we often would in James 4:3, which says, "When you ask you do not receive, because you ask with wrong motives, that you may spend what you get on your pleasures"? This passage clearly teaches us not only to be careful about what we pray for, but also that the root cause of not receiving answers to our prayers is the wrong motive.

Clearly, praying with wrong motives is not a new phenomenon. We humans simply appear bent on trying to perfect the practice, seemingly in the hope that doing a good job of perpetuating our errors will somehow improve on them. Those who prayed *just* to be known to pray are called hypocrites in Matthew 6:5:

> But when you pray, do not be like the hypocrites,
>   for they love to pray standing in the synagogues
>   and on the street corners to be seen by men.
>   I tell you the truth, they have received their
>   reward in full.

The pagans who think they will be heard simply because of their many words are referred to as "babblers" in verse 7. I'm afraid that people have had centuries of practice at misguided praying practices. But in order to move on successfully, first we need to know the answer to this question: What does it take, then, to get our prayers answered? Prayer is vital to Christianity. Without it, we don't express our dependence on God, nor do we indicate that we care about seeing His will done on earth. Consider the context of the comments preceding the Lord's Prayer in Matthew 6 (though it could be argued that John 17 is His prayer, and that Matthew 6 is a guideline for how we should pray). The prime considerations (i.e., the context) surrounding this well-known prayer include the following:

- the things we are taught to seek, from the Sermon on the Mount (Matthew 5:1–12)
- the concepts of Christians being salt and light, to God's glory (5:13–16)

- the need for righteousness that exceeds the demands of the law (5:17–20)
- the recognition of the spiritual truth that we are to be judged for our thoughts and motives (5:21–30)
- that faithfulness (5:31–32), integrity (5:33–37), submission (5:38–42), and love (5:43–48) are *actually* required of us
- that quiet giving (6:1–4), humility (6:5–8), proper attitudes to spiritual disciplines (6:16–18), a proper focus of our earnest attention (6:19–24), and a quiet confidence in God that relies on Him for the very basics of life itself, are all actually essential (6:23–34)

The essence of a vital (or even a reasonable) prayer life is outlined for us in the context of the prayer that Jesus, Himself, used as an example to teach us how to pray. Let's look first at the well-loved and respected teaching of Christ from the Sermon on the Mount (Matthew 5:3–12):

> Blessed are the poor in spirit, for theirs is the kingdom of heaven.
> Blessed are those who mourn, for they will be comforted.
> Blessed are the meek, for they will inherit the earth.
> Blessed are those who hunger and thirst for righteousness, for they will be filled.
> Blessed are the merciful, for they will be shown mercy.
> Blessed are the pure in heart, for they will see God.
> Blessed are the peacemakers, for they will be called sons of God.
> Blessed are those who are persecuted because of righteousness, for theirs is the kingdom of heaven.

> Blessed are you when people insult you, persecute
> you and falsely say all kinds of evil against you
> because of me.
> Rejoice and be glad, because great is your reward in
> heaven, for in the same way they persecuted the
> prophets who were before you.

Do you notice that what our Lord is instructing us to do has *everything* to do with our attitude and very little to do with our performance (or actions)? He did not lead us to believe that "blessed are the North Americans for they shall really put together some high-tech meetings." Nor did He declare, "Blessed are those who keep themselves in great shape, for they shall consider themselves really favored by God." The physical focus of our typical prayers is undeniably out of step with the focus of these scriptures. They teach that our attitude will determine our reward. We seem to be of the opinion that by our very asking, God owes us an answer as our reward. Think about what that implies. Do we *really* want to dare to be seen trying to manipulate the Sovereign God into a position of being obligated to us? *Who* is it that is sovereign, after all?

Consider only one example of these prayer topics: do you want security? Do we not normally regard security as financial stability and freedom from threat? How much security, stability, or freedom would you dare to pray for? How would you like to have the whole earth to share as your inheritance? If you would, the way to get it is not to pray specifically for security or finances, but pray for meekness of spirit (Matthew 5:5). How contrary this is to what we have come to observe as normal praying. Are not the inmost desires of our hearts to be met in the list of rewards offered in these few verses: heaven, comfort, an inheritance, fullness, mercy, and seeing God?

Continuing on, what do you notice are the emphases of these scriptural examples on prayer?

And when you stand praying, if you hold anything against anyone, *forgive him*, so that your Father in heaven may forgive you your sins. (Mark 11:25)

Repent of this wickedness and pray to the Lord. Perhaps he will forgive you for having *such a thought in your heart*. (Acts 8:22)

They devour widows' houses and *for a show make lengthy prayers*. Such men [those lacking in mercy] will be punished most severely. (Mark 12:40)

If you believe, you will receive whatever you ask for in prayer. (Matthew 21:22)

After they prayed, the place where they were meeting was shaken. And *they were all filled with the Holy Spirit* and spoke the word of God boldly. (Acts 4:31)

I pray that out of his glorious riches *he may strengthen you with power through his Spirit in your inner being*, so that Christ may dwell in your hearts through faith. (Ephesians 3:16–17a)

For this reason, since the day we heard about you, we have not stopped praying for you and asking God to fill you with the *knowledge of his will through all spiritual wisdom and understanding*. (Colossians 1:9)

> And this is my prayer: that *your love may abound*
> *more and more in knowledge and depth of insight.*
> (Philippians 1:9)

Did you find a commonality in these verses? Is it not the emphasis on the internal: the spiritual, mental, and emotional emphases of our attitudes, beliefs, and motivations; our internal values, if you will?

BALANCING PRAYER

While my desire here is to affirm the importance of the believer's attitude in prayer, certainly there are clear indications in the Bible that we *are* free (and in fact invited) to pray about physical things. The following scriptures provide some balance in that regard:

> I pray that you may be active in sharing your faith, so
> that you will have a full understanding of every
> good thing we have in Christ. (Philemon 1:6)

> Is any one of you sick? He should call the elders of
> the church to pray over him and anoint him
> with oil in the name of the Lord. And the prayer
> offered in *faith* will make the sick person well;
> the Lord will raise him up. If he has sinned, he
> will be forgiven. Therefore confess your sins to
> each other and pray for each other so that you
> may be healed. The prayer of a righteous man is
> powerful and effective. (James 5:14–16)

> Dear friend, I pray that you may enjoy good health
> and that all may go well with you, even as your
> soul is getting along well. (3 John 1:2)

> With this in mind, we constantly pray for you, that
> our God may count you worthy of his calling,

and that by his power he may fulfill every good
purpose of yours and every act prompted by
your faith. (2 Thessalonians 1:11)

God is interested in every aspect of our lives, and these few references are but a small sampling of His desires for us. My purpose in emphasizing our attitude toward spiritual things in our prayers is not to say that we shouldn't be praying about needed rain, health, or our business. My purpose is to remind each of us that, while these are legitimate concerns about which to pray, they are not likely intended to be the foundational issues of our prayers. The more important considerations are those I've previously highlighted, some very important things we may have missed.

You see, even in the times of the prophets, so often the actions of the people appeared to be beyond criticism, but their hearts were far from God. Perhaps they were even saying all the right words in their prayers. But they showed a lack of mercy, righteousness, justice, and love (Hosea 6:6; Micah 6:8; see also Revelation 2:1–7). It was for what was *lacking,* not what was being done, that they were criticized.

Doing right is not a prerequisite for a soundly effective prayer life. *Being* right is. What you are on the inside has complete sway over the legitimacy of your spirituality. Assuming that you are careful to ask according to God's will, your attitude does determine your reward, even in God's response to your prayers. Remember, the value of the content of the prayer matters little; God is aware of what you want before you even ask (Matthew 6:8). What God sees is the heart, including the attitude, motives, or whatever you call it, of the petitioner. This is what He responds to, not the bare words of the request alone.

Maybe you should read that paragraph again.

These other passages (chosen from the many in Scripture) reflect the importance of the heart attitude in prayer:

> And if they turn back to you *with all their heart and soul* in the land of their captivity where they were taken, and pray toward the land you gave their fathers, toward the city you have chosen and toward the temple I have built for your Name; then from heaven, your dwelling place, hear their prayer and their pleas, and uphold their cause. And forgive your people, who have sinned against you. (2 Chronicles 6:38–39)

> If my people, who are called by my name, will *humble themselves and pray and seek my face* and turn from their wicked ways, then will I hear from heaven and will forgive their sin and will heal their land. (2 Chronicles 7:14)

> Let your ear be attentive and your eyes open to hear *the prayer your servant is praying before you day and night* for your servants, the people of Israel. I confess the sins we Israelites, including myself and my father's house, have committed against you. (Nehemiah 1:6)

> So I turned to the Lord God and *pleaded with him in prayer and petition*, in fasting, and in sackcloth and ashes. (Daniel 9:3)

> *Do not be anxious* about anything, but in everything, by prayer and petition, *with thanksgiving, present your requests to God.* (Philippians 4:6)

For this reason, since the day we heard about you, we have not stopped praying for you. We continually ask God to fill you with the knowledge of his will through all the wisdom and understanding that the Spirit gives, and we pray this in order that you may live a life worthy of the Lord and may please him in every way: bearing fruit in every good work, *growing in the knowledge of God.* (Colossians 1:9–10)

I want men everywhere to lift up holy hands in prayer, without anger or disputing. (1 Timothy 2:8)

The LORD is far from the wicked but he hears the prayer of the *righteous.* (Proverbs 15:29)

Husbands, in the same way be considerate as you live with your wives, and treat them with *respect* as the weaker partner and as heirs with you of the gracious gift of life, so that nothing will hinder your prayers. (1 Peter 3:7)

But you, dear friends, *build yourselves up in your most holy faith and pray in the Holy Spirit.* (Jude 1:20)

For the eyes of the Lord are on the righteous and his ears are attentive to their prayer, but the face of the Lord is against those who do evil. (1 Peter 3:12)

The end of all things is near. Therefore *be clear-minded and self-controlled so that you can pray.* (1 Peter 4:7)

> And being in anguish, he prayed more earnestly, and his sweat was like drops of blood falling to the ground. When he rose from prayer and went back to the disciples, he found them asleep, exhausted from sorrow. "Why are you sleeping?" he asked them. "Get up and *pray so that you will not fall into temptation.*" (Luke 22:44–46)

Now, look at what results from right praying:

> *As soon as you* began *to pray, an answer was given*, which I have come to tell you, for you are highly esteemed. Therefore, consider the message and understand the vision. (Daniel 9:23)

> Therefore I tell you, whatever you ask for in prayer, *believe that you have received it, and it will be yours.* And when you stand praying, if you hold anything against anyone, *forgive* him, so that your Father in heaven may forgive you your sins. (Mark 11:24–25)

It is demonstrably true that God intimately connects our attitude in prayer with His response to that prayer. Uprightness, holiness, earnestness, faith, and self-control are only a few of the requisite standards that must hold sway in our lives. It is apparent that here, our faith is expressed in effectual, fervent prayers that accomplish much (James 5:16).

If this is the case for our prayer lives, it is at least as much so for our worship, for how can we hope to come into His presence in praise without the right attitude?

4

Worship and the Believer

There are many ways to worship. In whatever you choose to do in worship, my hope and prayer is that you will do it intentionally and thoughtfully, to honor the one who is so very, very worthy.

When was the last time you were in a worship service, where you honestly believed that the whole body of believers gathered there were worshipping genuinely? In most meetings that are designated as a worship service, some people may display the spirit of worship, but have you noticed that people are rarely involved in true, corporate worship, where almost everyone present is actually worshipping? If you were to stand at the back of your church at any given worship service and look around the room at each person there, what would you see? If your observations parallel those of many other believers, then you might admit that few people are involved in significant, universal corporate biblical worship of our great God. Lots of people seem to be just standing there.

I expect that this situation arises for many and varied reasons. For some, it may be a simple misunderstanding of what worship is. Others may be unable to enter into the experience because of a spiritual problem. For many, a cultural block may prohibit their involvement. I'd like us to briefly consider each of these possibilities.

MISUNDERSTANDING WORSHIP

This word is generally acknowledged to have been derived from *worthship*, an archaic English word. The connection is quite obvious; it is recognizing worth. It includes reflecting on God Himself and offering to Him praise and exaltation for who He is. It is recognizing that the one we call God really is God, that He is Master, Lord, Supreme, Sovereign, the Holy Other of space and of time and of eternity, and (most specifically) of my life, as well. It is having the *perspective* of these examples of scriptural worship (be particularly attentive to the words and phrases printed in italics, as the emphasis is mine):

> And when they heard that the LORD was concerned about them, and had seen their misery, they *bowed down* and worshiped. (Exodus 4:31)

(This was after the Israelites first learned of God's willingness to save them from their bondage in Egypt.)

> "So now I *give* him to the LORD. For his whole life he will be given over to the LORD." And he worshiped the LORD there. (1 Samuel 1:28)

(This was upon Hannah's presentation of her son, Samuel, to God, for His service.)

> Yet a time is coming and has now come when the true worshipers will worship the Father in *spirit and truth,* for they are the kind of worshipers the Father seeks. God is spirit and his worshipers *must* worship in spirit and in truth. (John 4:23–24)

(Notice that it isn't that He'd really like it if we worshipped him in spirit and truth, but that that we *must* worship Him that way.)

> Therefore, I urge you, brothers, in view of God's mercy, to *offer your bodies* as living sacrifices, holy and pleasing to God—this is your spiritual act of worship. Do not conform any longer to the pattern of this world, but *be transformed by the renewing of your mind.* Then you will be able to test and approve what God's will is— his good, pleasing and perfect will. (Romans 12:1–2)

> *Sing* to the LORD, all the earth; *proclaim* his salvation day after day. *Declare* his glory among the nations, his marvelous deeds among all peoples. For great is the LORD and most worthy of praise; he is to be feared above all gods. For all the gods of the nations are idols, but the LORD made the heavens. Splendor and majesty are before him; strength and joy in his dwelling place. *Ascribe* to the LORD, O families of nations, ascribe to the LORD glory and strength, ascribe to the LORD the glory due his name. *Bring an offering* and come before him; worship the LORD in the splendor of his holiness. (1 Chronicles 16:23–29)

> *Give thanks* to the LORD, for he is good; his love endures forever. *Cry out,* "Save us, O God our Savior; gather us and deliver us from the nations, that we may give thanks to your holy name; that we may *glory in your praise.* Praise be to the LORD, the God of Israel,

from everlasting to everlasting." Then all the people said "Amen" and "Praise the LORD." (1 Chronicles 16:34–36)

Therefore, since we are receiving a kingdom that cannot be shaken, let us *be thankful,* and so worship God acceptably with *reverence and awe,* for our God is a consuming fire. (Hebrews 12:28–29)

These references, along with others, point out a significant but sometimes missing ingredient in contemporary worship services. That key ingredient is the attitude of the worshiper that results in appropriate action. We seem not to have a solid grasp of the vital importance of our mind-set as we enter into a worship opportunity. You see, I believe that worthship must apply to what we offer as well. Our worship must be worthy of the God to whom we present it.

One does not worship simply because the Sunday morning bulletin says this is a worship service. We truly worship only after we have a clear understanding of

- what it is that we are supposed to be, and
- what we are supposed to be thinking, and then actively engage our understanding and our being as worshipers.

Only then can we know what we ought to be doing. I'm afraid we often have this backward (perhaps if we do all the right things, it will help us to think properly: fake-it-till-you-make-it-type behavior), or else we just skip any consideration of the motive at all and move directly to the action. Why? Well, what do you think? Maybe it's just easier for us to go through the motions rather than to be bothered with analyzing and correcting our attitudes. Of course, this approach is easier, but it's also faulty.

This perspective leads us to examine a second possible reason why some may not truly enter into a worship experience: there may be a spiritual problem that prevents us from being able to worship God.

SIN AS A BARRIER TO WORSHIP

In order for you to relate to God, there must be an open channel of communication between you and God. Sin blocks this channel. You cannot be out of fellowship with God and expect to be able to get anything out of, or contribute anything to, worship. Ponder the weight of 1 John 1:5–10:

> This is the message we have heard from him and declare to you: God is light; in him there is no darkness at all. If we claim to have fellowship with him yet walk in the darkness, we lie and do not live by the truth. But if we walk in the light, as he is in the light, we have fellowship with one another, and the blood of Jesus, his Son, purifies us from all sin. If we claim to be without sin, we deceive ourselves and the truth is not in us. If we confess our sins, he is faithful and just and will forgive us our sins and purify us from all unrighteousness. If we claim we have not sinned, we make him out to be a liar and his word has no place in our lives.

Sin, then, is a genuine separator. This is further substantiated in Psalm 66:18, which reads, "If I regard iniquity in my heart, the Lord will not hear." The solution to the dilemma is simple, yet devastating. Simple, because it is God, Himself, who has chosen to make the path between us clear again, by providing forgiveness for our sins, if we ask Him to. It is devastating, because it requires us, in fact, it *demands* us, to admit to being wrong. Since Adam and Eve (and Cain and Abel), this has been one of the most difficult things for a human to do.

One of our greatest sins is still pride. Pride keeps us from forgiveness; it keeps us living on as defeated Christians (perhaps all the while singing "The Greatest Thing in All the World Is Serving You"*). How foolish we are. Can't we believe God? Can't we see that we are just repeating the errors of those judged so harshly in Scripture? Galatians 3:1–3a chastises those of us in the present, as surely as it did the Galatians centuries ago:

> You foolish Galatians! Who has bewitched you? Before your very eyes Jesus Christ was clearly portrayed as crucified. I would like to learn just one thing from you: Did you receive the Spirit by observing the law, or by believing what you heard? Are you so foolish? After beginning with the Spirit, are you now trying to attain your goal by human effort?

Yes, we *do* try to attain our goal by human effort, all the time. This has seemingly become standard practice. It has resulted in the weakening of dozens of Christian denominations, missions, and parachurch agencies across the globe. We have become accustomed to saying that we rely on God but deny Him the right of Lordship in our lives.

Does this directly affect our worship? Of course. Does it affect everything else we do as believers? Yes, just as surely. Transgressing this single scriptural directive and doing things our own way probably causes more ineffective (yet so-called spiritual) activity than almost anything else we can think of.

Why, then, do we persist in following this lame and impotent path of action instead of allowing God to work through us His preferred path of likeness? Are we not supposed to be like Him?

Surely we know that we, as humans cannot do what He does, yet we insist on trying to justify ourselves by our actions, all the while refusing to admit that there's anything wrong. Perhaps we don't even recognize that we, ourselves, are living in the midst of dreadful times, like those we are warned about in 2 Timothy 3:1–8

> But mark this: There will be terrible times in the last days. People will be lovers of themselves, lovers of money, boastful, proud, abusive, disobedient to their parents, ungrateful, unholy, without love, unforgiving, slanderous, without self-control, brutal, not lovers of the good, treacherous, rash, conceited, lovers of pleasure rather than lovers of God—*having a form of godliness but denying its power.* Have nothing to do with them. They are the kind who worm their way into homes and gain control over weak-willed women, who are loaded down with sins and are swayed by all kinds of evil desires, always learning but never able to acknowledge the truth. Just as Jannes and Jambres opposed Moses, so also these men oppose the truth—men of depraved minds, who, as far as the faith is concerned, are rejected.

How accurately does this list describe our current global culture? An amazing parallel, isn't it?

But back to justifying ourselves: how often do we pride ourselves on being the group who is true to God. It's the others (you know which ones) who call themselves Christians but who don't really believe the Bible; they're the ones these verses describe. We have the sound doctrine. Even if it were true that our doctrine is good, our obedience to Scripture may be no better than theirs. May God help us. Remember Matthew 7:1–5:

> Do not judge, or you too will be judged. For in the same way you judge others, you will be judged, and with the measure you use, it will be measured to you. Why do you look at the speck of sawdust in your brother's eye and pay no attention to the plank in your own eye? How can you say to your brother, "Let me take the speck out of your eye," when all the time there is a plank in your own eye? You hypocrite, first take the plank out of your own eye, and then you will see clearly to remove the speck from your brother's eye.

We who point fingers so self-righteously are practicing a form of godliness but denying its power, as Paul warned us would happen. Are we not prone to judging others harshly, even unjustly, but then turning right around and excusing ourselves?

Dear friend, let's go back to 1 John 2 and continue on in the passage we began earlier (verses 1–6):

> My dear children, I write this to you so that you will not sin. But if anybody does sin, we have one who speaks to the Father in our defense—Jesus Christ, the righteous one. He is the atoning sacrifice for our sins, and not only for ours but also for the sins of the whole world. We know that we have come to know him if we obey his commands. The man who says, "I know him," but does not do what he commands is a liar, and the truth is not in him. But if anyone obeys his word, God's love is truly made complete in him. This is how we know we are in him: Whoever claims to live in him must walk as Jesus did.

May God help us to recognize the pit in which we are allowing ourselves to remain. He detests pride; so should we, in others, perhaps, but first and most notably in ourselves. Is there any form of pride that is more arrogant than acting as though "I'm fine; it's really those others who need to get right with God."? Repentance is often needed but seldom practiced, unless we get caught. My friend, we're caught. The God who sees and knows all, judges the intents of the heart, not our performance or our attendance. Do you now begin to understand that you simply cannot worship with sin, of any description, in your life? It *will* separate you from God. By not confessing it, you choose to remove yourself from fellowship with the one who gives life meaning and purpose. No wonder we get frustrated or picky about trivialities like the music, the lighting, or the message.

Cultural Barriers to Worship

A third reason for not managing well in a worship setting may, in fact, be cultural. Can you picture anyone in your congregation behaving like some of the examples in the scriptures listed early in the chapter, like crying out in sackcloth and ashes? Does the average person at your church bow down, bring an offering while crying out, offer his body as a living sacrifice, or even come in reverence or awe? Instead, don't people come into the sanctuary chatting about their week, the game, their latest purchase? Would the members of your fellowship be quieter and better behaved (or more joyful and exuberant) if a president, prime minister, or celebrity were to be present than if it's just God who's there? Be honest. If necessary, be hard on yourself. It would be my guess that most of us would be more in awe of a visiting dignitary than we are of God's presence. We *know* this isn't right, but my guess is that it's also accurate.

I understand that it may not be culturally appropriate to bow down and cry out in church these days, and that's not at all what I'm promoting. But what about the culturally appropriate things we do that seem to be in contravention of God's Word? For example, have you ever been in a conservative church where a worship song was sung that contained lyrics like "I lift up holy hands in your name," and no one did? To some, this may be a cultural thing. They do it, and we are the conservatives, and we don't want to be accused of being like them, so we don't lift our hands. Instead, we may do one of three things: we commit this action to a heart attitude rather than a physical action; we stand there and mouth meaningless gibberish; or at the worst, we lie to our Lord. Consider Psalm 134 and 1 Timothy 2:8:

> Praise the LORD, all you servants of the LORD who minister by night in the house of the LORD. Lift up your hands in the sanctuary and praise the LORD. May the LORD, the Maker of heaven and earth, bless you from Zion.

> I want men everywhere to lift up holy hands in prayer, without anger or disputing.

These verses suggest that this is something that we *ought* to do, and clear examples of it as a practice include Nehemiah 8:6 and Psalm 28:2, 63:4, and 119:48. If we had only these examples, it could possibly be argued that this, too, is a cultural situation in which, at that point in history, they practiced raising their hands before God. Even if it were the case that raising the hands before God may have been purely cultural, for us to now stand before God and declare that we do something when, in fact, we have no intention of ever doing it is to misunderstand the concept of being judged, by God, for every idle, empty, or careless word we utter. Would not such actions and words come under some degree of condemnation then?

Matthew 12:36 says that we will have to give account for every idle or careless word we have spoken. Might it be wiser to refrain from singing than to possibly be judged for uttering something that you know you have no intention of doing? Perhaps the worship leader should alter the lyrics to "lift my eyes" or "lift my heart." Just some thoughts.

This seems like a good place to remind you of my opening paragraph: There are a number of ways of worshipping. If you sincerely believe that you are lifting up holy hands in your heart and need not do so physically, that is between you and God. I do not criticize your choice. My purpose here is not to make anyone refrain from worship because of anything I write. My purpose is to encourage each of us to engage in worship and to seriously evaluate anything that may be coming between us and the one who alone is worthy of our worship. True worship is a delight to God and to the worshipper. It is not to be undervalued.

This brings us to the concluding observations in this chapter, based on 1 Corinthians 14:15 and Matthew 12:36, which follow:

> So what shall I do? I will pray with my spirit, but I will also pray with my understanding; I will sing with my spirit, but I will also sing with my understanding.

> But I tell you that everyone will have to give account on the day of judgment for every careless word they have spoken.

I believe that participants in Christian worship services (and in life in general) have an obligation to actually think, to concentrate. For example, how often do we sing songs of consecration when we have absolutely no serious thought about surrendering our all to God? Is it really more important to be seen singing than to be truthful before God?

Or, worse yet, are you asked to sing out (really raise the roof) when singing something, rather than being warned that you will be judged by God for your sincerity? Brothers and sisters in Christ, what do you think this scripture means? Is it not plain and straightforward? Or do you think that maybe God will just forget about this one? After all, you're sincere about your faith in Jesus as Savior, and that's what counts most, isn't it?

No. What counts most is your acceptance of Jesus as Lord. His being Savior is a wonderful blessing; there's no question about that. But your relationship with Jesus, and with the world, will be evaluated by your acknowledgment of him as Lord, the one who is in charge of your life, the unquestioned, supreme master of your thoughts, words, actions, and motives. Is that what He is to you right now? If you're looking for help, here it is: Acknowledge Jesus Christ as the genuine and active Lord of your life. Do it now. But at any cost, make sure that He is the unchallenged master of your entire being. May God help us all to understand that this is what faith expressing itself in love is all about. It is the life of the Living God being expressed back to Him and to the world.

(A note to worship leaders here: please take your role seriously. It is more important that those in your care understand, than that they sing out loudly. Please put their souls before their performance.)

I want to offer some biblical support for this idea. Consider two poignant selections of the Holy Scriptures: "All men will know that you are my disciples, if you love one another" (John 13:35). This indicates that our attitude toward each other may be fairly evaluated by others to determine the validity of our claim to have a genuine relationship with Jesus Christ.

And Hebrews 4:12–13: "For the word of God is living and active. Sharper than any double-edged sword, it penetrates even to dividing soul and spirit, joints and marrow; it judges the *thoughts and attitudes of the heart.* Nothing in all creation is hidden from God's sight. Everything is uncovered and laid bare before the eyes of him to whom we must give account."

These verses clearly set forth how believers will be judged. He who knows everything—what you've done, what you've neglected to do, what you've said and thought in your most private moments, your motives for service, your thoughtfulness during worship and prayer—will judge you based on your thoughts and attitudes. Nothing, therefore, could be more important to be certain about than this: what are you on the inside? What are you allowing yourself to become? What is your *real* relationship with the sovereign, Creator God of the universe? And what are you doing with or about that relationship? See also 1 Corinthians 4:1–5 (faithfulness); Mark 7:6–8 (avoid the teachings of men only); Ephesians 4:22–24 (be made new in the attitude of your mind); and Revelation 2:23b (God searches the heart and mind).

One final thought about church culture: Does your group have any way of *evaluating* your church programs? And if you do, are you exercising that faithfully? For example, someone suggests a program that serves the unreached in your community because this is what they're looking for in a church. Does anyone in your group dare to stand up and ask, "How do you know? Have you asked them?" I personally believe that we do an awful lot of guessing as to what someone else wants without ever asking them. For example, you might consider trying a simple neighborhood blitz with questions like:

- What do you expect church to look and sound like?
- Would you go to a church that looks and sounds like that?
- What would you like church to look and sound like?
- If XYZ Church looked and sounded like what you like, would you come regularly?

Their answers may surprise you. They may *expect* church to look and sound like a traditional church, and you finally threw away the hymn books. Or they may say that they'd *like* it if it looked and sounded like the neighborhood pub, but they wouldn't come anyway, even if you changed it to what they just said they'd like. The point is, maybe we should quit guessing and try to be better stewards of the resources and instructions that our Lord has committed to us.

A second problem that often rears its head is thoughtlessly buying into a program just because it's heavily promoted. Just because someone else says it's fabulous (or even if it works somewhere else) doesn't mean it will work in your congregation (e.g., music arranged for solo recording artists may *not* be the best for congregations to sing). There is value in thinking contextually about ministry. Just saying ...

* "The Greatest Thing in All the World"
    Words and Music by Mark Pendergrass
    © 1977 Universal Music - Brentwood Benson Songs (Admin. by Brentwood-Benson Music Publishing, Inc.)
    Candle Company Music (Admin. by Capitol CMG Publishing)
    Sparrow Song (Admin. by Capitol CMG Publishing)

5

Serving God

"Christian service" is an important concept. It's often recognized as an indicator of our dedication to Christ. It was even a requirement for graduation at colleges I've attended.

This chapter is aimed at helping each of us, as individuals, in our quest towards becoming. It is not intended that we evaluate someone else to actually grade their spirituality, nor to excuse our own lack thereof. Understanding that premise, then, read on.

I want to follow two thoughts here: how we value what is done; and whether we value *why* it is done. First, the what, but prefaced by a request: be completely honest in answering these questions. My aim here is not to prove any particular point, but, rather, to remind each of us of the validity and value of a position which adheres to the Word of God, which I trust we are attempting to discover. (Besides, you have nothing to lose. You're probably reading this book by yourself, so who else but God will know your thoughts, anyway?) May God grant you His grace in abundance as you continue on.

At the outset, I should acknowledge that all viable Christian service is the work of ministering the life of Christ to the body of Christ and to the world at large. This normally happens through the work of the Holy Spirit in the believer through the combination of the exercise of the fruit of the Spirit (Galatians 5:22–23) and the gifts of the Spirit (Romans 12:6–8; 1 Corinthians 12:4–11, 12:28). Any attempt to serve God without being rooted and carried out in the power of God will surely come to naught at best.

To begin with, then, in your opinion, who are the ten most important people in your congregation? (Now, please go with me on this. Do the exercise in this paragraph before going on to the rest of this chapter.) Literally write these names down the left side of a sheet of paper. Beside each name attempt to write words or short phrases that describe why you believe they are among the more significant individuals in your group. After you complete this list, rank these entries in descending order of importance. Who could you not get along without? Put this person as number 1, with the next most vital person as number 2, and so on through the list of ten. (Bear in mind that no one else will ever see or know about your list. Don't worry about who goes exactly where. If you can't decide on a ranking between two individuals, rate them as a tie. This is intended simply as an enlightening exercise, not as a theological statement or a trick question. Don't get hung up on it.)

What sorts of reasons did you give for evaluating each person's contribution? Read over your list. In your reasons column, have you listed things like "teaches my kids at youth group," "serves on the board," "gives heavily to the building program," or "is always faithful in attendance"? If most of your entries are like these sample points, you have probably ranked their contribution to the body in relation to the significance of their role or performance, in your opinion. It is quite customary for a list, such as you have just developed, to rank the pastor or ministering staff as number 1 or 2. This is simply signifying that to many people, their contribution is the most vital to the health and growth of that particular body of believers. But does that mean that the one who preaches is more significant to the body than someone who works in the church kitchen? Perhaps, but possibly only from a certain, limited perspective (which we will investigate more fully later).

What about your own contribution to the church? Did you put yourself on the list? If not, think for a moment about why not. Is it, in fact, because you actually *do* contribute less than others? Or is it that you are genuinely humble about your contribution to the development of the body of Christ? Or did you feel you could have put your own name down, but felt rather self-conscious about doing so? Well, it's up to you to determine the reason, but I'd like you to carefully think a bit more about your ranking as we move through this chapter.

So what do you believe about your Christian service? Where do you believe you fit? And while we're at it, do you feel that it is more spiritual, or more rewardable, to preach to a great congregation than to be a good church janitor? If you would rank yourself lower on the scale, is it because you don't think that your role is important enough to be higher on the list? If you taught a seminary prophecy class, would that be more spiritual than mowing the church lawn? Be honest. What do you really think? Do you live as though there are legitimate ranks in serving God or the church? How does your answer to this question square with the list you did earlier? Have you considered the more prominent or public ministries as more important than the less public ones? If so, why do you think you did that? Is it not because you believe that they truly *are* more important? Most of us do exactly this. Many of us, at the same time, still agree with the theological perspective of the equal value of all believers in the Lord's eyes. Why the distinctions, then? Why do we say we believe in the equal value of all believers, yet we are likely to rank the contributions of people based primarily on their public performance?

There are at least two possible explanations. First, while all believers are of equal value in God's sight, we value their contributions to the body differently because of the differences of the impact of their ministries on our lives. So those who build us up or lead us or teach us are appreciated and valued for that contribution. We value them out of gratitude and respect, and that ought not to be a problem. The danger that lurks behind this perspective is that there is more often a second, less appropriate reason for valuing those in public ministries more highly than others. And that is that we tend to equate their spiritual vitality with certain levels of activity.

If the key people in a congregation are those who are heavily involved, it may in fact be that they *are* the ones who are the spiritual leaders. It may also only be because they are the ones who serve on the boards and committees, teach children, work with clubs or the youth groups, or participate in the music programs. These people are often considered key because they are among the most faithful at Sunday services, and a few of them form the core of the other significant ministries of the church. They are held in esteem by others in the fellowship and are regarded as the "pillars of the church." Are you asking, "Do you have a problem with that?" Answer: No, unless we are regarding people as leaders solely by virtue of their involvement. This involvement could be their financial ability to support the work, their role in the group, or any other consideration, above the primary biblical requisite for church leadership, which is true biblical spirituality.

Allow me to offer what I perceive to be some key scriptures in this regard. Let me first preface this by saying that I recognize that "man looks at the outward appearance, but the LORD looks at the heart" (1 Samuel 16:7). But I would be unfair if I did not balance this with equally true scriptures observing that the eligibility for leadership includes qualifications that are more than performance-based.

To begin with, Hebrews 13:17 tells us that leaders should enjoy their work, but that their responsibilities are great:

> Obey your leaders and submit to their authority. They keep watch over you as men who must give an account. Obey them so that their work will be a joy, not a burden, for that would be of no advantage to you.

Other than enjoying their ministry, what should characterize those of us who serve Christ? Weigh the significance of each of these additional scriptures:

> Am I now trying to win the approval of men, or of God? Or am I trying to please men? If I were still trying to please men, I would not be a *servant of Christ*. (Galatians 1:10)

Seeking God's approval over man's is one way to characterize those who serve Christ.

> Then the leaders of families, the officers of the tribes of Israel, the commanders of thousands and commanders of hundreds, and the officials in charge of the king's work gave *willingly*. They gave toward the work on the temple of God five thousand talents and ten thousand drams of gold, ten thousand talents of silver, eighteen thousand talents of bronze and a hundred thousand talents of iron. Any who had precious stones gave them to the treasury of the temple of the LORD in the custody of Jehiel the Gershonite. The people rejoiced at the *willing response* of their leaders, for they had given *freely and wholeheartedly* to the LORD. David the king also rejoiced greatly. (1 Chronicles 29:6–9)

Here, the leaders set the example in giving willingly.

> An elder must be *blameless,* the husband of but one wife, a man whose children believe and are not open to the charge of being wild and disobedient. Since an overseer is entrusted

with God's work, he must be blameless—not overbearing, not quick-tempered, not given to drunkenness, not violent, not pursuing dishonest gain. Rather he must be *hospitable, one who loves what is good, who is self-controlled, upright, holy and disciplined.* He must hold firmly to the trustworthy message as it has been taught, so that he can encourage others by sound doctrine and refute those who oppose it. (Titus 1:6–9)

In this passage, the leader's home life and teaching are to be exemplary.

To the elders among you, I appeal as a fellow elder, a witness of Christ's sufferings and one who also will share in the glory to be revealed: Be *shepherds* of God's flock that is under your care, serving as overseers—not because you must, but because you are *willing,* as God wants you to be; not greedy for money, but *eager to serve,* not lording it over those entrusted to you, but being examples to the flock. (1 Peter 5:1–3)

The attitude of willing servanthood must be exhibited.

And this is my prayer: that your *love* may abound more and more in knowledge and depth of insight, so that you may be able to *discern* what is best and may be *pure and blameless* until the day of Christ, *filled with the fruit of righteousness* that comes through Jesus Christ—to the glory and praise of God. (Philippians 1:9–11)

Discernment and purity leading to a life of righteousness is required.

> As a prisoner for the Lord, then, I urge you to *live a life worthy of the calling you have received.* Be *completely humble and gentle; be patient, bearing with one another in love. Make every effort* to keep the unity of the Spirit through the bond of peace. (Ephesians 4:1–3)

Live a life of humble support for the family of God.

> If anyone considers himself religious and yet does not keep a *tight rein on his tongue,* he deceives himself and his religion is worthless. (James 1:26)

Clean speech should be normal.

> But the *wisdom* that comes from heaven is first of all *pure;* then *peace-loving, considerate, submissive, full of mercy and good fruit, impartial and sincere.* Peacemakers who sow in peace raise a harvest of righteousness. (James 3:17–18)

Leaders live to make the peace of God real in the lives of others.

> Love must be *sincere.* Hate what is evil; cling to what is good. Be *devoted to one another in brotherly love. Honor* one another above yourselves. Never be lacking in *zeal,* but keep your *spiritual fervor,* serving the Lord. *Be joyful in hope, patient in affliction, faithful in prayer. Share* with God's people who are in need. *Practice hospitality.* Bless

those who persecute you; bless and do not curse. *Rejoice with those who rejoice; mourn with those who mourn.* Live in *harmony* with one another. Do not be proud, but be *willing to associate with people of low position.* Do not be conceited. Do not repay anyone evil for evil. Be *careful* to do what is right in the eyes of everybody. If it is possible, as far as it depends on you, live at *peace with everyone.* For the kingdom of God is not a matter of eating and drinking, but of *righteousness, peace and joy in the Holy Spirit,* because anyone who serves Christ in this way is *pleasing to God and approved by men. (*Romans 12:9–18)

These leaders and servants live with loving hospitality to all, offering joy and hope to everyone in Jesus's name.

Let us therefore make every effort to do what leads to *peace and to mutual edification. (*Romans 14:19)

They build up and encourage.

The end of all things is near. Therefore be *clear minded and self-controlled* so that you can pray. Above all, *love each other deeply,* because love covers over a multitude of sins. *Offer hospitality* to one another without grumbling. Each one should use whatever gift he has received to *serve others, faithfully administering God's grace* in its various forms. If anyone speaks, he should do it as one speaking the very words of God. If anyone serves, he should do it with the strength

> God provides, so that in all things God maybe
> praised through Jesus Christ. To him be the
> glory and the power for ever and ever. Amen.
> (1 Peter 4:7–11).

Recognize the shortness of time available to serve others, and use every opportunity to be gracious.

Look again at the list you developed at the beginning of this chapter. Have you selected words to describe worthy Christians that are like those highlighted in the above passages? Have you included adjectives like "gracious," "forgiving," "peaceful," or "self-controlled"? Does your list focus primarily on performance-oriented attributes, or does it list mostly attitudes? The answers you give will indicate two things: first, the qualifications most obvious to you are predominantly of one kind or the other; second, the attributes you value most are primarily of one kind or the other. If you are like the majority of people who do this exercise honestly, you'll likely have listed more performance-based qualities than you will have character qualities. This is a reflection of one of the significant weaknesses of the Christian church at this point in our history; while not meaning to be insensitive, we seem to be unaware of how to even value biblical spirituality.

We are often unable to clearly recognize what characterizes a true, biblically spiritual individual. What does one look like, sound like, or behave like? It seems that we all too often look only to actions to define the term. For example, suppose someone was confronted by another believer for some apparent failing in his or her life. If the individual breaks into tears, says he or she should have done better, asks for your forgiveness, is *this* a truly spiritual person?

Suppose another believer is careful to present a good image by always appearing friendly and conciliatory: the mild-mannered Clark Kent type. Is *this* a spiritual individual? If a church leader hasn't spoken to another member of the congregation for years because of an earlier misunderstanding, but is otherwise a great supporter of the work, is he even qualified to be in leadership? How many are still active in your church? "But we really need him" (some might say).

On the other side of the coin, if Christians are unexcitedly straightforward about their preaching or teaching, are they not spiritual? Or if they occasionally miss a public service to spend time with their family, are they backsliders? I trust that no further examples are necessary.

Of course, the answer to each of these questions is probably much the same: "We just can't tell from that information alone." Tears don't make a changed life. Pleasant speech won't atone for manipulative motivations. The occasional personality conflict may be just that, though it could possibly indicate a more deeply-rooted problem. Similarly, the lack of an emotional display or absence at services can't indicate a lack of true spirituality, either. Upon what, then, can we rely to determine who it is that we can follow, believe in, or trust as a Christian leader? How do we verify biblical spirituality?

I believe that we must fundamentally trust our Lord, for He is ever and always what we desire and need Him to be. And we must want to be like Him, through His grace and Spirit. Beyond this most wonderful truth, we can trust His Word, and those who demonstrate the appropriate attitudes of Christ, some of which are to be found in the italicized words and phrases in the passages we studied earlier in this chapter. My friends, we can't rely on tears, service, agreeable speech, or any other external aspect of personality, because these have very little to do with the heart attitude. They may just as easily reflect years of good acting or self-deception.

Those who are fit to serve are those who are redeemed; who want to serve Christ and His body; who enjoy it; who live consistent lives of integrity; and who consistently exhibit the gentle, loving attributes of Jesus Christ by the power of His Holy Spirit living within them. Dare I suggest that such leaders will be those you observe to be truly living out their faith as they express it in love.

Most importantly, may God help each of us to not only value and cherish these people but become such a person ourselves, by God's gracious working in us. This should be the aim of each of us as we conclude this chapter. Then there will be the spiritual leaders the church needs; they will be you and me, by God's grace.

The desire to be such a believer will then lead us to the consideration of a major factor in our own spiritual development: our personal motivation.

6

Motivation

I believe that the statement "Attitude determines response" is largely true. As you genuinely believe, you will normally act. Yet it seems to be very easy for each of us to declare something as important to us, but appear not to live accordingly. Why? I think the root problem is our mind-set, our focus, that which is at the very core of our operational presuppositions. The Bible clearly illustrates this for us in Psalm 26:2: "Test me, O LORD, and try me, examine *my heart and my mind.*"

> I the LORD *search the heart and examine the mind,*
>   to reward a man according to his conduct,
>   according to what his deeds deserve. (Jeremiah
>   17:10)

These verses parallel the New Testament declaration of Jesus, in Luke 10:27. He answered,

> Love the Lord your God with *all your heart* and
>   with all your soul and with all your strength
>   and with *all your mind* and, Love your neighbor
>   as yourself.

Similarly, in Romans 12:2, Paul said,

> Do not conform any longer to the pattern of this world, but *be transformed by the renewing of your mind.* Then you will be able to test and approve what God's will is—his good, pleasing and perfect will.

It is so encouraging to know that the Lord's wisdom never fails. He recognizes that our motives and attitudes are ultimately represented in our speech, not necessarily in our carefully constructed public speaking, but more often in our private comments or conversations, even in our self-talk. Have you not found this to be borne out in your own life? All too often, what is thought or said in our own minds is not what would honor the Lord but would bring shame to Him and to ourselves, were it known. The heartbreak is this: it is known.

Remember, in chapter 1, I referred to 1 Chronicles 28:9, where we were reminded that "the LORD searches every heart and understands every *motive* behind the thoughts." The lie we seem to have bought into is that we can get away with tolerating occasional (or habitual) trash on the inside, as long as we think that no one will find out. Part of the purpose of this book is to point out that this pattern of thinking misses the very essence of Christianity, for it is what we are on the inside that truly matters. Your actions amount to nothing if your attitude is not right before God. But be encouraged; there is hope. Integrity can be experienced, or a righteous God would not ask it from His children. His judgment is certain—true—but it is also fair in light of the resources He has graciously provided for us.

Let Hebrews 4:12–16 be refreshing to your memory and soul:

> For the word of God is living and active. Sharper than any double-edged sword, it penetrates even to dividing soul and spirit, joints and marrow; it judges the *thoughts and attitudes* of the heart.

Nothing in all creation is hidden from God's sight. Everything is uncovered and laid bare before the eyes of him to whom we must give account. Therefore, since we have a great high priest who has gone through the heavens, Jesus the Son of God, *let us hold firmly to the faith* we profess. For we do not have a high priest who is unable to sympathize with our weaknesses, but we have one who has been tempted in every way, just as we are—yet was without sin. Let us then approach the throne of grace with confidence, *so that we may receive mercy and find grace to help us* in our time of need.

The solution for us is this: No matter what we do, say, or think, it seems to be rewardable if done 1) in Christ, 2) by faith, and 3) with right attitudes and motives. Conversely, it is subject to condemnation if done 1) outside of Christ, 2) without faith, 3) or from the wrong motive or with an inappropriate attitude. My dear friend, do you grasp that this includes literally everything? Allow me to elaborate on each of these three points.

First and foremost, we must be in Christ. By this, according to the Bible, I mean that we must be true, Bible-believing, born-again followers of Jesus Christ as both Savior and Lord (John 3:14–15). Nothing else will get you to square one. To claim to trust Him as Savior and not acknowledge Him as Lord is to miss the point of faith and salvation. The issue is not whether you want to go to Heaven when you die or not. Who wouldn't? The real issue is, who is master over your life? The one who controls your life is the one you actually trust. If it's you, you're trusting yourself. If it's Jesus, then you're genuinely trusting Him. Do you remember hearing that you cannot serve two masters (Matthew 6:24)? Either you are with Him or you are against Him (Luke 11:23). There is no middle ground.

Second, whatever you do must be based on faith. This includes your service for God. At the end of Romans 14:23b, we read, "Everything that does not come from faith is sin." If you preach without faith, according to this verse, you're not serving God; you're sinning. (Ooh, that's harsh.) If you serve on a board or committee without faith, it is not ministry for Christ; it is sin. Do you recall the verse about us being judged for every careless word (Matthew 12:36)? How much more severe do you expect our judgment will be if we're found to have been intentionally disobeying God's will by pretending to do things for Him, when in fact, we knew that our heart was not right before Him? Is this not the most serious consideration we could have in life, after recognizing Jesus as Lord? Judge for yourself what God's Word tells us about the importance of our attitudes, as recorded in 1 John 5:1–8:

> Everyone who believes that Jesus is the Christ is born of God, and everyone who loves the father loves his child as well. This is how we know that we love the children of God: by loving God and carrying out his commands. *This is love for God: to obey his commands.* And his commands are not burdensome, for everyone born of God overcomes the world. This is the victory that has overcome the world, even our faith. Who is it that overcomes the world? *Only* he who believes that Jesus is the Son of God. This is the message we have heard from him and declare to you: God is light; in him there is no darkness at all. If we claim to have fellowship with him yet walk in the darkness, we lie and do not live by the truth. But if we walk in the light, as he is in the light, we have fellowship with one another, and the blood of Jesus, his Son, purifies us from

all sin. If we claim to be without sin, we deceive ourselves and the truth is not in us.

Third, we must deal with our motives, our attitudes, what we really are inside. Evaluate your position in light of these verses. This must be dealt with. We dare not deceive ourselves, hoping that everything will be all right (for without doubt, we are not deceiving God). We simply cannot, in light of scripture, expect that God will accept what we say more than He judges what we've been. What then is the hope? Can anyone be saved from this situation (Mark 10:26–27)? Certainly, for with God, all things are possible.

But does it still seem humanly impossible to you that anyone could live like this? In one way, I hope it does. For if so, you've grasped a fundamental truth of Christian living: if any human could do it, God's intervention would be unnecessary. If there were any way for us to reach God by our own efforts, Jesus would not have had to die. But he did die, after most earnestly praying, "My Father, if it is possible, may this cup be taken from me. Yet not as I will, but as you will," (Matthew 26:39) to pay the penalty for your sins. He died by His own choice, for *your* benefit. So no, there is no other way. Essentially, there is nothing in the Christian life that you can do by yourself. Total dependence on God is the only way to live a truly Christian life, for in its very essence, living as a believer is impossible for humans to do alone. Only God can live a completely Godly life, but He wants (and is fully able) to live that life in and through you; not a revised version of your previous life. God is not interested in making a better you. You're a dirty, stinking sinner. He's interested in making you into a beautiful, clean child of God, a new creation, one born of the Holy Spirit (2 Corinthians 5:17).

This is why what you believe and think—your motivations and attitudes—are what matter most to God. He is not primarily seeking your superb performance. He is seeking your total dependence and trust. He is looking for internal evidence of that most personal of emotions, your love: your love for Him and for other people here on this earth. The evidence? You will willingly bear one another's burdens (Galatians 6:1–3); you will not judge each other anymore (Matthew 7:1–2); and you will love each other, for all the world to notice (John 13:35).

How do you get to this point? The same way you get saved. But you mustn't think of this as a one-time decision, as we often regard the salvation decision. Salvation depends on your recognition of Jesus Christ as both Savior and Lord; so does viable Christian living. But living is clearly ongoing, progressive.

- You begin by recognizing that you have failed (and who among us hasn't?).
- You then seek God's forgiveness by faith, for that is all important. You admit that you are totally unable to fulfill even the most basic of God's expectations of you as a believer (such as loving Him with your whole being, loving your neighbor as yourself, loving your spouse as Jesus loves the church, praying without ceasing, and so on; we looked at these verses in chapter 5).
- You conclude by inviting God to, *in fact*, live His life through you, by His indwelling Holy Spirit, just as He intended in the first place.

Be encouraged by 1 John 1:9–10:

> If we confess our sins, *he is faithful and just* and will forgive us our sins and purify us from all unrighteousness. If we claim we have not sinned, we make him out to be a liar and his word has no place in our lives.

Notice that the issue here is not whether God and His Word have first place in our lives or not. He makes it clear: If we claim that we have not sinned, He has *no* place in our lives. Don't make

God out to be a liar. There is probably very little that any human being could do that would be more foolish than that. Rather, let God's Word have its rightful place in your life right now and for the rest of your life. Live openly, transparently, before Him. Live solely by His grace and mercy, led and empowered by His Word and His Holy Spirit, whose temple you actually become when you are born into his family.

Reflect again on the resurrection power, as given to us in Colossians 3:1–2:

> "Since, then, you have been raised with Christ, *set your hearts* on things above, where Christ is, seated at the right hand of God. *Set your minds* on things above, not on earthly things. For you died, and your life is now hidden with Christ in God."

It should be clear already that the key to living a biblically spiritual life is the Holy Spirit, the actual presence of God living in *you*.

- Titus 3:5 declares that we are saved through "the washing of rebirth, and renewal by the Holy Spirit."
- You are His temple (1 Corinthians 6:19–20); therefore, "Honor God with your body."
- 1 Thessalonians 4:8 tells us that it is God who gives us the Holy Spirit so that we are able to receive instruction.
- One of the greatest selections on Christian living is in Ephesians 4, where we are told not to grieve the Holy Spirit because it is in Him that we are sealed for the day of redemption.

Stated plainly, our salvation, the power to live in this corrupt world, our ability to understand godly instruction, and our security are all because of the work of the Holy Spirit in our lives. Every part of our faith is sustained by His holy presence. Thank God for choosing to leave His loving presence within us. No wonder that Paul can encourage us to live out our faith. He is the author who reminds us of the presence of the Holy Spirit living in us, allowing us to know, experience, and express God's love to those around us.

7

Christian Growth

As Michael and Jen thought more about their church, their feelings were mixed. They had been treated well there. They had grown in their faith, more at first than lately, but they had sort of figured that this was the way it would be, and that made them wonder why. Wasn't it possible to keep growing? Is that what happened to some of their friends? Had they all just quit growing in Christ? Is that what must be the norm for believers, that they should level off in their actual spiritual development and only continue to grow in their knowledge?

What have been your own, personal observations in this regard? Are you happy with your growth rate into the "whole measure of the fullness of Christ" (Ephesians 4:13)? If not, why not? Why do you suppose you've not grown as you think you might, or should, or would like to? Do you think that others are more advanced in their faith than you are? If they truly are, why might this be the case? But if they aren't doing much better, then perhaps there is a problem common to many of us. If that is the situation, could we help each other in some way?

This might be the most frustrating part of our Christian walk for those who are believers to contemplate: our own lack of genuine, sustained development in Christ. I don't accept that God wants stunted, baby believers. The principles and guidelines He has given us make that which seems the norm unnecessary. Thank God for His Word. We turn to it again for His help for His beloved children to grow.

At the outset, it seems unfortunately accurate to state that not all who profess to come to Jesus as Savior will continue to live lives that reflect growth. This is to be expected, based on the parable of the sower and the seed, found in Matthew 13, Mark 4, and Luke 8. In each case, the meaning of the parable is given. Here is the Luke account (verses 4-15):

> A farmer went out to sow his seed. As he was scattering the seed, some fell along the path; it was trampled on, and the birds of the air ate it up. Some fell on rock, and when it came up, the plants withered because they had no moisture. Other seed fell among thorns, which grew up with it and choked the plants. Still other seed fell on good soil. It came up and yielded a crop, a hundred times more than was sown.

> When he said this, he called out, "He who has ears to hear, let him hear."

> His disciples asked him what this parable meant. He said, "The knowledge of the secrets of the kingdom of God has been given to you, but to others I speak in parables, so that, 'though seeing, they may not see; though hearing, they may not understand.'

> "This is the meaning of the parable: The seed is the word of God. Those along the path are the ones

who hear, and then the devil comes and takes away the word from their hearts, so that they may not believe and be saved. Those on the rock are the ones who receive the word with joy when they hear it, but they have no root. They believe for a while, but in the time of testing they fall away. The seed that fell among thorns stands for those who hear, but as they go on their way they are choked by life's worries, riches and pleasures, and they do not mature. But the seed on good soil stands for those with a noble and good heart, who hear the word, retain it, and by persevering produce a crop."

We have already referred to some of the destructive works of the devil. Here, he is seen snatching the very Word of God from the first group—unbelievers—so that they may not believe and be saved. He continues to be active in the same way today.

The second group are people who begin well, seemingly with full intentions of living for God, but when the difficulties of life come along, they assume their faith is no longer working. Because of their doubt or for some other reason, they abandon their faith. They are lacking in sufficient grounding in the Word to have their faith made strong. They haven't developed deep personal roots that go down into Scripture, nor do they have a significant background of positive experiences with God. They have nothing to feed on and nothing to look back to as encouragement (see 1 Samuel 7:12).

This is strictly speculation, but my guess is that the third group may be the largest. It seems that very little derails a Christian as easily as these concerns: worry, riches, and pleasure. Do you struggle in one of these areas? Do you have difficulty fully trusting God to care for every aspect of your life? Or do you find it necessary to sometimes take over for Him, by assuming the control of your own affairs?

Perhaps it's a financial concern that separates you from your spiritual growth potential. Maybe you're more concerned with the growth of your investments, properties, retirement savings, or income than you should be.

Maybe you wrestle with your own enjoyment. Is it more pleasurable for you to go golfing or camping than it is to go to Sunday services? Would you, in fact, rather work late than go to a prayer gathering (though you may publicly protest having to do so)? These are not the only reasons for a person becoming a choked-out believer, but they are representative of the types of things that tend to separate us from fellowship with God.

Is worry a necessary evil? Can any of us avoid this seemingly universal pitfall? Is there a line to be drawn between acting responsibly and not trusting God properly? If so, how do we determine where to draw this line in any given situation? Aren't there too many predicaments in life to have a rule for each one? What does God expect us to trust Him for, and what does He expect us to do for ourselves?

We'll discuss each of these three topics later in this chapter, for they are of great significance to the believer. Bear in mind, it is our Lord Jesus, Himself, who is giving us this instruction directly, so we need to deal with these concerns ("as they go on their way they are choked by life's worries, riches and pleasures" are Jesus's own words).

So many questions. But real life isn't simple, is it? Real life is messy. We *do* have questions. It's just that we are sometimes afraid to ask them, for fear that God might think we are questioning our faith. Recall, once again, that we are dealing with the one who already knows our thoughts, including our questions. He isn't going to be surprised if you voice what He already knows you are wondering about. Besides that, if your faith can't stand up to your own questions, what makes you think it will stand up to anyone else's? (Or is this why you don't witness as you feel you ought? Perhaps, deep down, you don't really think that your faith can stand up to close scrutiny or questioning.)

My dear friend, faith in the one true God of the Bible can take it. How could the Almighty Creator be God, by definition, if He were unable to remain so under investigation? God, in fact, openly invites us to be involved with Him at the deepest levels of searching. He summons us in these most cordial ways, by the testimony of King David:

> *I sought the LORD, and he answered me*; he delivered me from all my fears. Those who look to him are radiant; their faces are never covered with shame. *This poor man called, and the LORD heard him*; he saved him out of all his troubles. The angel of the LORD encamps around those who fear him, and he delivers them. Taste and see that the LORD is good; blessed is the man who takes refuge in him. Fear the LORD, you his saints, for those who fear him lack nothing. The lions may grow weak and hungry, but those who seek the LORD lack no good thing. Come, my children, listen to me; I will teach you the fear of the LORD. Whoever of you loves life and desires to see many good days, keep your tongue from evil and your lips from speaking lies. Turn from evil and do good; seek peace and pursue it. *The eyes of the LORD are on the righteous and his ears are attentive to their cry.* (Psalm 34:4–15)

Consider also the Father's own request, as recorded in Isaiah 1:18:

> *"Come now, let us reason together,"* says the LORD. "Though your sins are like scarlet, they shall be as white as snow; though they are red as

crimson, they shall be like wool. If you are
willing and obedient, you will eat the best from
the land; but if you resist and rebel, you will be
devoured by the sword." For the mouth of the
LORD has spoken.

Add to these the words of Jesus:

Come to me, all you who are weary and burdened,
and I will give you rest. Take my yoke upon you
and *learn from me*, for I am gentle and humble
in heart, and you will find rest for your souls.
For my yoke is easy and my burden is light.
(Matthew 11:28–30)

Evidently God *does* want us to question, to investigate, to learn,
to know, but within the parameters of seeking Him. However,
He has made it equally clear that we are not to question Him
inappropriately. For example, Isaiah 29:16 says,

You turn things upside down, as if the potter were
thought to be like the clay! Shall what is formed
say to him who formed it, "He did not make
me." Can the pot say of the potter, "He knows
nothing"?

This analogy is continued in Isaiah 45:9:

Woe to him who quarrels with his Maker, to him
who is but a potsherd among the potsherds on
the ground. Does the clay say to the potter,
"What are you making?" Does your work say,
"He has no hands"?

While God obviously desires for us to know Him, it is just as obvious that we are not to question His authority to do with us as He pleases. We are His possession. He both created us and redeemed us. We are twice His. In this context, we need only to remember that Romans 8:28 says, "And we know that *in all things* God works for the good of those who love him, who have been called according to his purpose."

WORRY

Having established, then, that it is reasonable to question appropriately, let's continue our investigation. How may we know whether we are simply acting as responsible stewards when we question or whether we are indicating a lack of trust in God?

The first thing we ought to concern ourselves with is to determine whether we are honestly questioning or just using this as a diversion to hide our lack of true faith. This is critical, for if we just *pretend* to be seeking God's leading through our questions, it is simply a sham in order for us to be able to say "There, I asked God, and He didn't say I couldn't, so …" Once again, as is the thrust throughout this book, the difference is clearly one of motives and attitude. How do you know if your question is valid? Very simply, you know by your reason for asking it.

> Each of us knows our own heart. We fully understand that it is naturally deceitful above all things and beyond cure. Who can understand it? I the LORD search the *heart* and examine the *mind,* to reward a man according to his conduct, according to what his deeds deserve. (Jeremiah 17:9–10)

Armed with this recognition, we need to test our reason for asking. Are we seeking to justify ourselves? God alone can justify

(Romans 5). Are we looking for permission to take control of a situation ourselves? If so, perhaps we are not trusting God as we should be. Colossians 3:15–17 instructs us to:

> Let the peace of Christ *rule* in your hearts, since as members of one body you were called to peace. And be thankful. Let the word of Christ *dwell* in you richly as you teach and admonish one another with all wisdom, and as you sing psalms, hymns and spiritual songs with gratitude in your hearts to God. And *whatever you do*, whether in word or deed, do it all in the name of the Lord Jesus, giving thanks to God the Father through him.

Also, in 1 Thessalonians 4:1–3, we read:

> Finally, brothers, we instructed you how to live in order to please God, as in fact you are living. Now we ask you and urge you in the Lord Jesus to do this more and more. For you know what instructions we gave you by the authority of the Lord Jesus. *It is God's will that you should be sanctified.*

If our questions arise out of a lack of trust, they are inappropriate and a challenge to God's authority. If they are from a pure heart, with the honest desire to learn and discern God's will, they are valid. But above everything else, there must be that degree of integrity of heart and mind that allows us to be free before the Lord to ask the questions. Any distrust of the supremacy of God is invalid and subject to His judgment. To distrust demonstrates worry, which is simply our taking on the responsibility to control the situation in our own strength, without allowing God to exercise His right of control, as Lord. To conclude, it's the attitude of the questioner that counts more than the question itself.

WEALTH

"Oh, this part doesn't apply to me. I don't have any." Is that what you're thinking? Trust me, it applies.

We in the Western world (where most of my readers reside) tend to view wealth as relative, usually in one of two ways: either it's a relative who's wealthy or we don't feel wealthy, in relation to others. Well, rich uncles aside, what are the concerns of the wealthy? And how do these affect our walk with Christ that could cause us to grow cold in our relationship with Him?

Most people reading this book are reasonably secure, financially. By that, I mean they have enough nourishing food to sustain them, a reasonably safe roof over their head, and a fairly adequate wardrobe that allows them freedom of movement in their environment. Now, you may not dine on gourmet fare at each meal, you may not live in a palace, and you may not always wear the latest designer labels. Compared to the hundreds of millions on this globe—including other Christians—who have none of the benefits that most of us enjoy, we aren't too badly off. (By the way, if you do feast regularly, live in a palace, and wear designer clothes, this topic is still of concern to you and your spiritual development.) But most of us probably don't regard ourselves as wealthy, do we? I submit that this view may be, in part, because of our tendency to look at our own situation in comparison to others.

Human nature being what it is (corrupted), we tend to regard our assets as not as significant as somebody else's and our faults as not as bad as somebody else's. Do you grasp the thought here? We very rarely look at the absolute reality of a position; we more often tend to look at its relative reality. It will usually be true that, compared to another, you may not be as wealthy, talented, good looking, or whatever. But what is your real condition? Do you have just enough of this world's goods for the average non-North American to live on? Probably not. In most cases, we have considerably more than others in the world. The problem is that it feels like we never have enough to satisfy us. "Well, I'd be satisfied if …"

It's been said that if you cannot live within your means, you'll never have enough. I think that's probably true. We see evidence of it all around us. We all know families that have a reasonable income, but they always claim to be broke. You may ask what some of your acquaintances do with their money. People may ask this about you and me. What am I getting at? Two things: First, you likely have enough to get by on, if you have your giving, spending, and saving in proper balance (unless you either haven't maintained this balance and now find yourself in financial difficulty or had to face an unforeseen disaster). Second, that the things that concern the really rich people (whoever they are) generally concern the rest of us too.

The really wealthy are often concerned about the stability of their income, the acquisition of goods or properties, establishing a sense of security for their future, protecting their assets, and so on. However, these considerations are common to most of us, not just those we regard as really rich; these concerns may, in fact, occupy *more* time in the minds of those who are poorer than those who don't have to think about these matters because they know their financial needs are cared for.

Our Lord's point in the parable of the seed and the sower is that concerns over the everyday affairs of trying to get by will cause us to be choked out in the struggle for an active faith. The reason is probably obvious to us all: Our attention is focused on our life situation instead of on the Lord Jesus. Our gracious and loving Savior is just reminding us to focus on Him and then allow Him to care for us, as the scriptures indicate:

> Do not store up for yourselves treasures on earth,
>   where moth and rust destroy, and where thieves
>   break in and steal. But store up for yourselves

treasures in heaven, where moth and rust do not destroy, and where thieves do not break in and steal. For where your treasure is, there your heart will be also. The eye is the lamp of the body. If your eyes are good, your whole body will be full of light. But if your eyes are bad, your whole body will be full of darkness. If then the light within you is darkness, how great is that darkness! No one can serve two masters. Either he will hate the one and love the other, or he will be devoted to the one and despise the other. You cannot serve both God and money.

Therefore I tell you, do not worry about your life, what you will eat or drink; or about your body, what you will wear. Is not life more important than food, and the body more important than clothes? Look at the birds of the air; they do not sow or reap or store away in barns, and yet your heavenly Father feeds them. Are you not much more valuable than they? Who of you by worrying can add a single hour to his life?

And why do you worry about clothes? See how the lilies of the field grow. They do not labor or spin. Yet I tell you that not even Solomon in all his splendor was dressed like one of these. If that is how God clothes the grass of the field, which is here today and tomorrow is thrown into the fire, will he not much more clothe you, O you of little faith? So do not worry, saying, "What shall we eat?" or "What shall we drink?" or "What shall we wear?" For the pagans run after all these things, and your heavenly Father

> knows that you need them. *But seek first* his
> kingdom and his righteousness, and all these
> things will be given to you as well. Therefore do
> not worry about tomorrow, for tomorrow will
> worry about itself. Each day has enough trouble
> of its own. (Matthew 6:19–34)

Isn't the Bible amazingly practical when we allow it to be? God is saying that without His blessing, you can't do anything right anyway, so trust Him. In reality, could there possibly be any better way than to trust the concerns you have over money to the sovereign Lord of lords and King of kings? This truth is actually awesome in its scope and practicality. Seek, *in the first place, His kingdom and righteousness,* and all these things will be given to you as well (Matthew 6:33).

PLEASURE

What about pleasure? I think that here, we might all be in trouble. Not because we Christians aren't supposed to have any pleasure, for that surely is false, but because we each derive our pleasure from doing so many different (often very good) things. By way of illustration, remember the fellow from Michael's church who worked in the shop that he and Chris ran? It seemed to Chris that this fellow got pleasure out of at least two things: listening to off-color stories and acting holier-than-thou. He wanted to be in on the bad while displaying his good.

People often have a perverted view of pleasure. They may think of pleasure as something we shouldn't have. Pleasure is sometimes mistakenly thought of as whatever is forbidden. I offer a contrary view. Psalm 37:4 teaches you to "delight yourself in the LORD, and He will grant you the desires of your heart." Interestingly, this passage clearly teaches us that if we get our delight priority correct, our desires will come along, and our delight is to be in the Lord. My opinion of the pleasures of the scriptures we'll consider is that they are often anything that the believer craves more than God. Let me say that again: I consider that inappropriate pleasures are anything you want or enjoy more than you enjoy God.

This certainly would include all of the forbidden pursuits, such as illicit sex, overeating, drinking to excess, and so on. This could also be your work. Perhaps it's never being wrong. It might be your opinion of yourself. It could even be your desire to be perceived by others as spiritual. Stop and think about that for a minute. Now, I certainly don't have all the answers; the truth is, I probably have very few. But I do have some concerns, and one of them is this: What must *I* do in order to enjoy God more than anything else? Ask yourself the questions I am asking myself (and You might as well be honest with yourself; God knows what you're thinking right now anyway, right?)

- Do you enjoy your work more than you really enjoy God?
- Do you enjoy ministry—serving Him—more than you actually enjoy Him?
- What *do* you enjoy most? (Make another list, if that will help you.)
- Which of those things you've listed, whether good or bad, do you enjoy more than you enjoy God?
- Or do you actually prefer all of them to Him?
- In your opinion, could that make even the good ones at least questionable?
- Do you think you ought to do something about that?
- What will the price of holiness be for you?
- Are you willing to let God change what you think you ought to change?

Does the concept of pleasure that I am presenting here seem reasonable to you? As I asked earlier, would you rather be camping or golfing than gathering with other believers? Perhaps you're thinking, *I've worked hard. I deserve this. We'll go back in the fall.* What about the work Jesus did for you (He offered Himself to be crucified)? Did He deserve that? What about the instruction of Scripture in Hebrews 10:24–25:

> And let us consider how we may spur one another on toward love and good deeds, not giving up meeting together, as some are in the habit of doing, but encouraging one another—and all the more as you see the Day approaching.

Is it plausible that the God who created and redeemed you should want your first desire to be for Him? Just look at how the Lord so intrinsically combines our love for Him with demonstrations of our loyalty:

> Hear, O Israel: The LORD our God, the LORD is one. Love the LORD your God with all your heart and with all your soul and with all your strength. These commandments that I give you today are to be upon your *hearts*. Impress them on your children. Talk about them when you sit at home and when you walk along the road, when you lie down and when you get up. Tie them as symbols on your hands and bind them on your foreheads. Write them on the door frames of your houses and on your gates …

> Fear the LORD your God, serve him only and take your oaths in his name. Do not follow other gods, the gods of the peoples around you; for the LORD your God, who is among you, is a jealous God and his anger will burn against you, and he will destroy you from the face of the land. Do not test the LORD your God as you

did at Massah. Be sure to keep the commands of the LORD your God and the stipulations and decrees he has given you. (Deuteronomy 6:4–9, 13–17)

The source of our most genuine joy and delight is to be our relationship with God, Himself. This has always been God's choice for His children, as attested to by David in Psalm 16:11 and by the beloved apostle, John, in chapter 15 of his book, in verses 9–12:

> You have made known to me the path of life; you will fill me with joy in your presence, with eternal pleasures at your right hand.

> As the Father has loved me, so have I loved you. Now remain in my love. If you obey my commands, you will remain in my love, just as I have obeyed my Father's commands and remain in his love. I have told you this so that my joy may be in you and *that your joy may be complete. My command is this:* Love each other as I have loved you.

For me, I think the most telling verses are those found in 2 Timothy 3:1–5:

> But mark this: There will be terrible times in the last days. People will be lovers of themselves, lovers of money, boastful, proud, abusive, disobedient to their parents, ungrateful, unholy, without love, unforgiving, slanderous, without self-control, brutal, not lovers of the good, treacherous, rash, conceited, lovers of pleasure rather than lovers

of God—*having a form of godliness but denying its power.* Have nothing to do with such people.

What can we be sure of? We affirm that our trust is to be indisputably in Him, freeing us from worry.

Our financial affairs are to be entirely under His direction, with us as stewards (managers) of all the resources committed to us (1 Corinthians 4:2).

The greatest pleasure we can identify in life is to delight in growing in our knowledge of Him and the fullness of His love and grace, which are both freely extended to us.

In short, the focus of our mind-set—our attitude—is to be centered on God alone, with every other aspect of life continuously rippling out from Him as the center.

8

The Will of God

After many years in ministry, I still struggle with what to say to someone in grief. Perhaps it's a terminal illness, the death of a loved one, some major loss or tragedy, or concern over an unsaved friend or family member. Whatever the situation is, the result is the same. The hurt, sorrow, and grief can only be known by the individual who is directly affected.

Another thing that causes me real distress during these times, is when another believer, seemingly wanting to be encouraging or helpful, says something like, "It must have been God's will" (that your baby died or you lost your job or your parent is suffering from some debilitating disease). Now, they may intend to affirm that God is sovereign and is in ultimate control of all that happens, but does that mean that God really wants babies to be burned in a tragic fire or children to be killed by a drunk driver or some frail senior citizen to be wracked with pain or humiliating dysfunction?

To me, though, the worst is when some tragedy occurs and a well-known Christian leader rises up and declares that God is judging the suffering group because of some sin. Can we see that leader's faith expressing itself through love in that situation?

Obviously, God judges sin. But He's also merciful, loving, just, and kind. How do we reconcile these two? No one would say that God wants evil to come into our lives, so what does it really mean that something is the will of God?

Before we delve into the answers to those questions, I'd like to propose two other scenarios. Many times, those of us in ministry are invited to join other opportunities to serve. There may even be several openings available at the same time. Once again, the question of God's will comes into consideration. Which should this person choose (if, in fact, any)? Is there a wrong place to serve Christ?

A parallel question often occupies the minds of seminary students who are looking toward their future ministry and life. Who should they marry? Where should they live? Should they be an electrician, a missionary, an accountant, or a pastor? All of these questions may be rolled into the one, greater query: Where do they fit in the plan of God? Or does such a plan even exist? And if they make a wrong choice now, are they derailed from God's will for the rest of their lives? Suppose they feel they should become missionaries but don't. Will they never again know the blessing of the Lord? Must they thereafter settle for second best? What is God's will, anyway?

I believe it may help our understanding of how we view God's will, to think of it as at least three distinct things, as we see it described in Scripture. It may not be particularly like the blueprint for a building or some other detailed and unalterable plan. Nor is it necessarily a program that each of us must discover and somehow fit into. And it is not necessarily as simple as His making everything happen that happens. But it does need to be thought about, for we are, indeed, expected to live in it. (See Ephesians 5:1–21, especially verse 17: "Therefore, do not be foolish, but understand what the Lord's will is.")

What, then, are some facets of God's will? There are His *decrees* (He says something and it happens); there are His *preferences* (what He would like to have happen); and there are those things that He *permits* (things that always work for the good of the true believer).

GOD'S DECREES

God is all-powerful; omnipotent, if you prefer. That means that He is fully able to do anything at all that He chooses (see Job 42:2 and Matthew 19:26). This control extends over creation and pagans, as well as His children. When God decrees something, it simply happens. There is no debate, no choice, no alternative plan. When He wills something to happen *by decree*, it happens. Period. (See Isaiah 14:24, 46:9–10.)

Some examples for our enlightenment include the following:

Creation

> And *God said*, "Let there be light," *and there was light*. (Genesis 1:3)

> And *God said*, "Let the water under the sky be gathered to one place and let dry ground appear." *And it was so.* (Genesis 1:9)

> Then *God said*, "Let the land produce vegetation: seed-bearing plants and trees on the land that bear fruit with seed in it, according to their various kinds." *And it was so.* (Genesis 1:11)

> And *God said*, "Let the land produce living creatures according to their kinds: livestock, creatures that move along the ground, and wild animals, each according to its kind." *And it was so.* (Genesis 1:24)

World Governments

> In the first year of Cyrus king of Persia, in order to fulfill the word of the LORD spoken by Jeremiah, *the LORD moved the heart of Cyrus king of Persia* to make a proclamation

throughout his realm and to put it in writing. (2 Chronicles 36:22)

Everyone must submit himself to the governing authorities, for *there is no authority except that which God has established.* The authorities that exist have been established by God. (Romans 13:1)

The king's heart is in the hand of *the LORD; he directs it* like a watercourse wherever he pleases. (Proverbs 21:1)

Unbelievers

I am the LORD, and there is no other; apart from me there is no God. *I will strengthen you, though you have not acknowledged me.* (Isaiah 45:5 about the King of Babylon)

"Do you refuse to speak to me?" Pilate said. "Don't you realize I have power either to free you or to crucify you?" Jesus answered, *"You would have no power over me if it were not given to you from above."* (John 19:10–11a)

For the Scripture says to Pharaoh: *"I raised you up* for this very purpose, that I might display my power in you and that my name might be proclaimed in all the earth." (Romans 9:17)

Predestination/Salvation

For he chose us in him before the creation of the world to be holy and blameless in his sight. In love, he predestined us to be adopted as his sons through Jesus Christ, in accordance with his pleasure and will. In him we were also chosen, having been predestined according to the plan of him who works out everything in conformity with the purpose of his will. (Ephesians 1:4–5, 11)

[God] who has saved us and called us to a holy life—not because of anything that we have done, but because of his own purpose and grace. *This grace was given us in Christ Jesus before the beginning of time...* (2 Timothy 1:9)

For you know that it was not with perishable things such as silver or gold that you were redeemed from the empty way of life handed down to you from your forefathers, but with the precious blood of Christ, a lamb without blemish or defect. *He was chosen before the creation of the world*, but was revealed in these last times for your sake. (1 Peter 1:18–20)

Men of Israel, listen to this: Jesus of Nazareth was a man accredited by God to you by miracles, wonders and signs, which God did among you through him, as you yourselves know. This man was handed over to you *by God's set purpose and foreknowledge*; and you, with the help of wicked men, put him to death by nailing him to the cross. (Acts 2:22–23)

Vic Delamont

GOD'S PREFERENCES

Salvation

Scripture clearly indicates that God would like some things to happen that don't necessarily come to pass. Does that surprise you? It won't after you think about it for a moment. God plainly "wills" that everyone should "come to repentance," and He is "not wanting anyone to perish" (2 Peter 3:9). Does that mean, because it is God's declared desire, that all will be saved and enter heaven, somehow? No, for the Bible clearly states that only those who, in repentance and faith, call on the name of Jesus Christ as Savior and Lord, through His grace alone, will be saved, as shown in these selections:

> Then they asked him, "What must we do to do the works God requires?" Jesus answered, "The work of God is this: to believe in the one he has sent." (John 6:28–29)

> Not everyone who says to me, "Lord, Lord" will enter the kingdom of heaven, but only he who does the will of my Father who is in heaven. Many will say to me on that day, "Lord, Lord, did we not prophesy in your name, and in your name drive out demons and perform many miracles?" Then I will tell them plainly, "I never knew you. Away from me, you evildoers!" (Matthew 7:21–23)

> Brothers, my heart's desire and prayer to God for the Israelites is that they may be saved. For I can testify about them that they are zealous for God, but their zeal is not based on knowledge. Since they did not know the righteousness that comes from God and sought to establish their own, they did not submit to God's righteousness.

Christ is the end of the law so that there may be righteousness for *everyone who believes*. Moses describes in this way the righteousness that is by the law: "The man who does these things will live by them." But the righteousness that is by faith says: "Do not say in your heart, 'Who will ascend into heaven?' (that is, to bring Christ down) or 'Who will descend into the deep?' (that is, to bring Christ up from the dead)." But what does it say? "The word is near you; it is in your mouth and in your heart," that is, the word of faith we are proclaiming: That if you confess with your mouth, "Jesus is Lord," and believe in your heart that God raised him from the dead, you will be saved. *For it is with your heart that you believe and are justified, and it is with your mouth that you confess and are saved.* As the Scripture says, "Anyone who trusts in him will never be put to shame." For there is no difference between Jew and Gentile—the same Lord is Lord of all and richly blesses all who call on him, for, "Everyone who calls on the name of the Lord will be saved." (Romans 10:1–13)

This aspect of the will of God is the most fundamental and rudimentary that there is for humankind. The universal availability of salvation is essential to the gospel, as presented in scripture. Anyone who calls on the name of the Lord will be saved. And God wants everyone to be saved. But it doesn't happen. Why? Because while He would *prefer* it to happen, He doesn't *make* it happen. Salvation must be a free choice, because the very nature of salvation is a voluntary change of command in the life of the recipient of that salvation. God does not decree that we must be saved.

Instead, he provides that we may be saved. It is His preference, but not a decree, and so what He may long for, doesn't necessarily happen. By His choice, He does not get His own will realized irresistibly. As foolish as it is, we can refuse God's gift of salvation, or, as tragic as it is, no one may ever tell the lost that He has provided for their salvation. In either case, the lost will die in their sins and be eternally separated from God and His blessing. We know John 3:16, but John 3:17–18 affirms this when it says,

> For God did not send his Son into the world to condemn the world, but to save the world through him. Whoever believes in him is not condemned, *but whoever does not believe stands condemned already because they have not believed in the name of God's one and only Son.*

Thankfulness

In addition to salvation, what else is God's will that doesn't necessarily happen? Our thankfulness, for one thing. Paul instructs us in 1 Thessalonians 5:16–18 that we should "be joyful always; pray continually; give thanks in all circumstances, *for this is God's will for you* in Christ Jesus." Unfortunately, few believers are always joyful, prayerful, and thankful in all circumstances, yet "this is God's will." Again, it is His desire, but it doesn't necessarily happen. Fundamentally, our fitting into God's preferred will is predicated on both His willingness to reveal it to us and our willingness and readiness to receive it.

Surrendering to His Will

We know that he wants us to discern His will, because Scripture plainly tells us so (1 Thessalonians 2:1–3a; John 7:16–17; Matthew 11:28–30).

We also understand that there are requirements for us to be in a position for knowing His will. For example, we must

- utterly surrender to God ("Offer your bodies as living sacrifices"),
- separate from worldliness ("Do not conform any longer to the pattern of this world"), and
- become spiritually-minded ("Be transformed by the renewing of your mind") (all from Romans 12:1–2).

1 John 2:15–18 also gives us important instruction in placing our values on things that matter. It says,

> Do not love the world or anything in the world. If anyone loves the world, love for the Father is not in them. For everything in the world—the lust of the flesh, the lust of the eyes, and the pride of life—comes not from the Father but from the world. The world and its desires pass away, but whoever does the will of God lives forever.

How do we maintain this spiritual mind-set or attitude? We start by understanding that the commitment of Romans 12:1–2 actually begins with the word, "Therefore" (i.e., all that Paul taught in the first eleven chapters of Romans). The generalization I would like to draw from this is to base your life as a believer on *all* of scripture, not just your favorite verses (2 Timothy 3:16–17). Step one, then, is to begin to really know God's Word. Read it daily. *Study it with the intention of applying it* to your thoughts, attitudes, behaviors, practices, and habits. (Philippians 4:4–9 is excellent.) And then follow up by testing if your desires, ambitions, thoughts, and plans line up with Scripture. Is God, through the Holy Spirit, giving you peace in your plans and decisions? Do godly counselors agree with your choices? Do providential circumstances give opportunity for your plans?

Pursuing Godliness

> Since, then, you have been raised with Christ, *set your hearts* on things above, where Christ is seated at the right hand of God. *Set your minds* on things above, not on earthly things. For you died, and your life is now hidden with Christ in God. When Christ, who is your life, appears, then you also will appear with him in glory.

> Put to death, therefore, whatever belongs to your earthly nature: sexual immorality, impurity, lust, evil desires and greed, which is idolatry. Because of these, the wrath of God is coming. You used to walk in these ways, in the life you once lived. But now you must rid yourselves of all such things as these: anger, rage, malice, slander, and filthy language from your lips. Do not lie to each other, since you have taken off your old self with its practices and have put on the new self, which is being renewed in knowledge in the image of its Creator. Here there is no Greek or Jew, circumcised or uncircumcised, barbarian, Scythian, slave or free, but Christ is all, and is in all. Therefore, as God's chosen people, holy and dearly loved, *clothe yourselves* with compassion, kindness, humility, gentleness and patience. Bear with each other and forgive whatever grievances you may have against one another. Forgive as the Lord forgave you. And over all these virtues *put on love*, which binds them all together in perfect unity. Let the peace of Christ *rule in your hearts*, since as members of one body you were called to peace. And be thankful.

Let the word of Christ *dwell in you richly* as you teach and admonish one another with all wisdom, and as you sing psalms, hymns and spiritual songs with gratitude in your hearts to God. And whatever you do, whether in word or deed, do it all in the name of the Lord Jesus, giving thanks to God the Father through him. (Colossians 3:1–17)

What are the typical, ongoing attitudes of people who pursue godliness?

- repentance (2 Peter 3:9)
- obedience to known truth (1 Peter 1:22–25)
- striving for holiness and sexual purity (1 Thessalonians 4:3–8)
- living as a good, respectful citizen (1 Peter 2:13–17)

Becoming Christ-Like

Be imitators of God, therefore, as dearly loved children and live a life of love, just as Christ loved us and gave himself up for us as a fragrant offering and sacrifice to God. For you were once darkness, but now you are light in the Lord. Live as children of light (for the fruit of the light consists in all goodness, righteousness and truth) and *find out what pleases the Lord*. Have nothing to do with the fruitless deeds of darkness, but rather expose them. For it is shameful even to mention what the disobedient do in secret. But everything exposed by the light becomes visible, for it is light that makes everything visible. This is why it is said: "Wake up, O sleeper, rise from the dead, and Christ will shine on you."

Be very careful, then, how you live—not as unwise but as wise, making the most of every opportunity, because the days are evil. Therefore do not be foolish, but *understand what the Lord's will is*. Do not get drunk on wine, which leads to debauchery. Instead, *be filled with the Spirit*. Speak to one another with psalms, hymns and spiritual songs. Sing and make music in your heart to the Lord, always giving thanks to God the Father for everything, in the name of our Lord Jesus Christ. Submit to one another out of reverence for Christ. (Ephesians 5:1–2, 8–21)

Some attributes of Christ-likeness should incorporate things like:

- humble submission (Philippians 2:1–11)
- fruit-bearing/reproduction (John 15:5)
- a spirit of gracious giving (2 Corinthians 8:1–7)
- praying in the Spirit (Romans 8:26–27)
- consistency (1 Thessalonians 5:16–18)

Living to God's Glory

Characteristics of a life lived to God's glory should include:

- remembering Christ in communion (1 Corinthians 11:23–26)
- good works aimed at bringing glory to God (Matthew 5:14–16)
- pursuing unity (Romans 15:5–6)
- daily activities reflecting God's glory (1 Corinthians 10:31)

For believers to know and live in God's will is to live according to His preferences for us. We truly honor God by desiring, seeking, and pursuing godliness, Christ-likeness, and His glory.

GOD'S PERMISSION

The third facet of the will of the Lord is comprised of those things He may or may not choose to happen, but which He allows. Included in this category of His will are all the effects of humankind living in a cursed environment, ever since the time of Adam's fall. There is evil in the world. There are also natural consequences to actions that are governed by what are sometimes called second causes. God is the first cause, in that He created and began the systems that we now recognize as normal in our world. The gravitational interactions between the earth and the moon that cause the tides; the cycle of precipitation and evaporation; and the laws of inertia and momentum are examples of these systems. It is important to recognize that God does not need to intervene in these systems in order for them to work. They are now examples of second causes; that is, they bring consequences to bear by their very operation.

For example, God does not need to cause a flood in Asia during monsoon season. The rains, predictably, will fall heavily, and some people and animals may lose their lives as flooding results. Those lost lives are not caused by God directly. He does not decree that some die. Rather, the deaths are a result of the consequences of a violent weather pattern that is an outworking of a natural process. In Ezekiel 18:32, God tells us that "I take no pleasure in the death of anyone."

Similarly, God may allow the tragedy of accidents, but that does not mean that He causes the accidents. He may allow illness and pain, but this does not mean that He causes that illness or pain. These things are most often the natural results of error or the corruption, decay, and decline of the health and strength of the human body since the curse entered our world as a result of original sin.

To assume that God does, in fact, control everything that happens (in the same sense in which He decrees something) is to make Him the source of evil, as well as of good. God has declared Himself to be purely good, with no hint of evil within His being (see 1 John 1:5, James 1:17, and Psalm 145). Elementary logic teaches us that a thing cannot both be and not be the same thing in the same sense at the same time. Neither can God be purely good and not purely good. It is a contradiction in terms and a logical impossibility. No, our Lord does not do evil, but He can allow it.

What are His purposes in the life of the believer?

> We know that *in all things* God works for the good
> of those who love him, who have been called
> according to his purpose. (Romans 8:28)

God has, throughout human history, retained the right and the power to use what we perceive as evil for His good purposes. In Genesis 50:20, Joseph told his brothers, "You intended to harm me, but God intended it *for good* to accomplish what is now being done, the saving of many lives."

Yet God's providence is always in effect, his care and his plan for his chosen children.

> The Son is the radiance of God's glory, and the exact
> representation of his being, *sustaining all things
> by his powerful word.* After he had provided
> purification for sins, he sat down at the right
> hand of the Majesty in Heaven. (Hebrews 1:3)

> He is before all things, and *in him all things hold
> together.* (Colossians 1:17)

> You alone are the LORD. You made the
> heavens, even the highest heavens, and all

their starry host, the earth and all that is on it, the seas and all that is in them. You give life to everything, and the multitudes of heaven worship you. You are the LORD God, who chose Abram and brought him out of Ur of the Chaldeans and named him Abraham. You found his heart faithful to you, and you made a covenant with him to give to his descendants the land of the Canaanites, Hittites, Amorites, Perizzites, Jebusites and Girgashites. You have kept your promise because you are righteous. (Nehemiah 9:6–8)

From one man he made all the nations, that they should inhabit the whole earth; and he marked out their appointed times in history and the boundaries of their lands. God did this so that they would seek him and perhaps reach out for him and find him, though he is not far from any one of us. For *in him we live and move and have our being.* As some of your own poets have said, "We are his offspring." (Acts 17:26–28)

We often bring this problem upon ourselves: we feel we need to come up with a reason for everything. One way that this shows up is when we declare a tragic event to be God's judgment, without knowing whether this is actually the case. This ascription can cause great grief and distress, as alluded to in the first page of this chapter. Hopefully, you now have a better understanding as to why that may be a dangerous stance to take.

In conclusion, God's will is not simple, nor can we mere humans ever fully understand it. In the area of free will, God has apparently chosen to limit the irresistibility of His will. In the area of natural consequences, God generally chooses to allow the effects of our living in a cursed environment, among sinful humans, to function in ways that we have come to describe as normal. He does all of this to bring people to Himself and to bring about ultimate good out of every situation for those who acknowledge him as Lord, in order that we might be reconciled to Him and genuinely praise Him for who He truly is: "God our Savior, who wants all people to be saved and to come to a knowledge of the truth" (1 Timothy 2:4).

9

Your Worldview and How It Affects You

By "worldview," I mean the way you look at things, how you approach life, your perspectives and presuppositions. You see, each of us has a position from which we view, evaluate, and respond to the various circumstances of life. This view is developed through our education, experiences, values, beliefs, exposure to social and cultural mores, and so on. Since no two individuals have had exactly the same experiences, no two of us will have exactly the same perspective on life. This is why two people can view the same set of facts and come to two completely different conclusions about them: creationists and evolutionists, for example. Their worldview (their presuppositions) completely colors their understanding of what those facts may actually mean.

There are many ways to define these many perspectives in our time, from secular humanism to New Age philosophy, but I have chosen to explore only two categories: self-centeredness and pragmatic materialism (although you may not call them by these names, I'm certain that you'll recognize their traits by the end of the chapter). I chose these two because they are insidious in our society and dangerous in their deceptive power.

SELF-CENTEREDNESS

All humans initially look at, evaluate, and respond to the world from the perspective of being self-centered. The Bible teaches us that we are all born as sinners (see Psalm 53:3; 1 John 1:8). Part of the sin nature within us is the desire to have all of our needs and wants met, where and when we want them met. If you don't feed a hungry infant soon after he discovers he's hungry, he'll let you know of his wishes, and loudly. Unfortunately, some people never seem to move past that stage. Their entire life is centered on themselves. To this person, others are seen to be of value only as much as they contribute to what he wants or needs or feels is owed to him. This lifestyle may be characterized by the expression "I have a right ..." These people are the entitled.

While we all expect infants to cry when they're hungry, if this mind-set continues, it can have many negative effects later on in life. Preschoolers may throw temper tantrums. Children may lie to avoid punishment. Teenagers may behave uncharacteristically in order to be accepted by their peers. Adults may cheat on their taxes to receive a larger refund. In each case, and in thousands more, the primary consideration is the protection, benefit, or exaltation of self.

You can easily recognize this trait in others. The Bible teaches us that self-centeredness is sin. Romans 7:18–20, 1 Corinthians 10:24, 1 John 2:15–16, and other passages adequately clarify this for us. The cure for self-centeredness is for individuals to choose to become God-centered. Unfortunately, choosing to become a Christian doesn't do away with our sin nature, and so we all struggle to one degree or another with how to be free from the demands of our own selfish nature.

What salvation *does* do for us, however, is to make it possible to change. Romans 6:6–7 says:

> We know that our old self was crucified with him so that the body of sin might be rendered powerless, that we should no longer be slaves to sin—because anyone who has died has been freed from sin.

The thought here is that we were co-crucified with Jesus. As He died, so our sin nature, and its unrelenting control over us, also died. We only need to appropriate this truth, and live in and for Him, thereby no longer being forced to live in or for sin.

This is summarized in verses 11 and 12, where Paul instructs us to "count [reckon] yourselves dead to sin but alive to God in Christ Jesus. Therefore do not *let* sin reign in your mortal body so that you obey its evil desires."

We are to make this a calculated decision, in the same way an accountant would record a financial transaction. Having counted or reckoned ourselves as being dead to sin, we are then to make the determined *choice* to not let sin reign in our lives.

In our pre-Christian state, Satan controlled our thoughts, our worldview. But as we come to trust Jesus Christ and His redeeming work alone for our salvation, we move into the Christian sphere, where the power of God's Holy Spirit can establish a new worldview within us. It is the Holy Spirit now living in us who gives us this power to choose.

It is having this power to choose, under God's grace, that sometimes throws us off. We think we sin because we have no choice. Scripture teaches us that this is just not the case. It plainly teaches us that we are accountable and that we sin because we choose to.

To accept this premise goes directly against our innate desire for self-protection. We see a difference between something that just happened and something we choose to do, and so we should.

The problem lies in our inability to own up to those things that we claim just happened, when they were really our choice (however inappropriate or poor that choice may have been). We'd rather claim to be a victim than admit to being a perpetrator.

However, we simply can't truthfully say that our sin was brought upon us by any outside force alone. It is true that the sin we fall into is brought about as a result of temptation. This temptation may come as a result of "the world, the flesh, or the devil," but it doesn't come from God. James 1 gives us these truths in verse 13–15 and following:

> When tempted, no one should say, "God is tempting
> me." For God cannot be tempted by evil, nor
> does he tempt anyone; but each one is tempted
> when, *by his own evil desire,* he is dragged away
> and enticed. Then, after desire has conceived, it
> gives birth to sin; and sin, when it is full-grown,
> gives birth to death.

We find it easy to blame our failure to live victorious Christian lives on our temptations. "If I just had better friends," "We live in a society that's just too promiscuous," "It wasn't my fault," "The government should never have allowed that." These sentiments were probably expressed by every generation from Noah to the present. For surely temptation has not only always been with us; all too often, it has won. No, the problem is not new or stronger temptations; the problem is Christians who fail to understand how to appropriate into real life, the belief that *God truly can do all that He says He can,* even in you or me. Do you know what the very next verses in James say?

> Don't be deceived, my dear brothers. Every good
> and perfect gift is from above, coming down
> from the Father of the heavenly lights, who does
> not change like shifting shadows. *He chose to*

> *give us birth through the word of truth,* that we
> might be a kind of firstfruits of all he created.
> (James 1:16–18)

Isn't that outstanding? Immediately on the heels of a depressingly true passage about our weakness and trouble in temptation, we read that God's Word instructs us to not be deceived. We are not to be taken in by those concerns, for the counterbalancing truth is that "every good and perfect gift [including the ability to overcome temptation] is from above, coming down from the Father of the heavenly lights." God, who *is* light, gives to us only that which is a good and perfect gift. What has He chosen as the gift? "Birth through the word of truth." What is to be our response to this word? Verse 22: "Do not merely listen to the word, and so deceive yourselves. Do what it says."

Let me summarize the impact of these considerations:

- Temptation has been part of the human experience since creation.
- We are not to be deceived as to what God gives us; it is only good.
- We are also not to deceive ourselves by thinking that just listening to, or understanding, or knowing the Word of God will benefit us. Only obedience will allow us to fulfill God's Word. And what are we to obey? Those things which are His commands.

WHAT ARE SOME OF HIS COMMANDS?

I have selected several passages of Scripture for your consideration. Each of them is a direct command of God, and each deals with a different aspect of His instructions to us, His children. As you read, notice how much emphasis is placed on our attitude, even in His commands. Take note of how our faith is to be expressed.

To Believe in and Love Jesus

> Dear friends, if our hearts do not condemn us, we have confidence before God and receive from him anything we ask, because we obey his commands and do what pleases him. And this is his command: *to believe in the name of his Son, Jesus Christ,* and *to love one another* as he commanded us. Those who obey his commands live in him, and he in them. And this is how we know that he lives in us: We know it by the Spirit he gave us. (1 John 3:21–24)

> Everyone who believes that Jesus is the Christ is born of God, and everyone who loves the father loves his child as well. This is how we know that we love the children of God: by loving God and carrying out his commands. This is love for God: to obey his commands. And his commands are not burdensome, for everyone born of God overcomes the world. *This is the victory that has overcome the world, even our faith.* Who is it that overcomes the world? Only he who believes that Jesus is the Son of God. (1 John 5:1–5)

> We accept man's testimony, but God's testimony is greater because it is the testimony of God, which he has given about his Son. Anyone who believes in the Son of God has this testimony in his heart. Anyone who does not believe God has made him out to be a liar, because he has not believed the testimony God has given about his Son. And this is the testimony: God has given us eternal life, and this life is in his Son.

He who has the Son has life; he who does not have the Son of God does not have life. I write these things to you who believe in the name of the Son of God so that you may know that you have eternal life. This is the confidence we have in approaching God: that if we ask anything according to his will, he hears us. And if we know that he hears us—whatever we ask—we know that we have what we asked of him. (1 John 5:9–15)

The cornerstone of the gospel is to believe in and love Jesus, as God. Surely, there is no attitude more important than this. It is the foundation of salvation, wholly provided by God's grace, through faith in Jesus Christ's death and resurrection.

Attitude versus Performance

Then some Pharisees and teachers of the law came to Jesus from Jerusalem and asked, "Why do your disciples break the tradition of the elders? They don't wash their hands before they eat!" Jesus replied, "And why do you break the command of God for the sake of your tradition? For God said, 'Honor your father and mother' and 'Anyone who curses his father or mother must be put to death.' But you say that if a man says to his father or mother, 'Whatever help you might otherwise have received from me is a gift devoted to God,' he is not to 'honor his father' with it. Thus you nullify the word of God for the sake of your tradition. You hypocrites! Isaiah was right when he prophesied about you: 'These people honor me with their lips, but their hearts are far from me. They worship me in vain; their

teachings are but rules taught by men.'" Jesus
called the crowd to him and said, "Listen and
understand. What goes into a man's mouth does
not make him 'unclean,' but what comes out of
his mouth, that is what makes him 'unclean.'"
Then the disciples came to him and asked, "Do
you know that the Pharisees were offended
when they heard this?" He replied, "Every plant
that my heavenly Father has not planted will
be pulled up by the roots. Leave them; they are
blind guides. If a blind man leads a blind man,
both will fall into a pit." Peter said, "Explain
the parable to us." "Are you still so dull?" Jesus
asked them. "Don't you see that whatever enters
the mouth goes into the stomach and then out
of the body? But the things that come out of the
mouth come from the heart, and these make a
man 'unclean.' For out of the heart come evil
thoughts, murder, adultery, sexual immorality,
theft, false testimony, slander. These are what
make a man 'unclean' but eating with unwashed
hands does not make him 'unclean.'" (Matthew
15:1–20)

Doing the right thing wasn't the problem. Their lack of *being*
right before God was what separated them from the God they
claimed to love and serve. The lesson here is that all evil words and
actions are the outworking of our being evil inside. The actions of
our lives are simply open manifestations of what we are.

Willingness to Give Up Anything and Follow Jesus
"Teacher, what good thing must I do to get eternal
life?" "Why do you ask me about what is
good?" Jesus replied. "There is only One who

is good. If you want to enter life, obey the commandments." "Which ones?" the man inquired. Jesus replied, "Do not murder, do not commit adultery, do not steal, do not give false testimony, honor your father and mother, and love your neighbor as yourself." "All these I have kept," the young man said. "What do I still lack?" Jesus answered, "If you want to be perfect, go, sell your possessions and give to the poor, and you will have treasure in heaven. Then *come, follow me.*" When the young man heard this, *he went away* sad, because he had great wealth. Then Jesus said to his disciples, "I tell you the truth, it is hard for a rich man to enter the kingdom of heaven. I tell you, it is easier for a camel to go through the eye of a needle than for a rich man to enter the kingdom of God." When the disciples heard this, they were greatly astonished and asked, "Who then can be saved?" Jesus looked at them and said, "With man this is impossible, but with God all things are possible." (Matthew 19:16–26)

This precious teaching of our Lord not only assures us that the wealthy can be saved, it also teaches us that a spirit of willing submission is superior to obeying all of the previously recognized commandments. Remember, Jesus did not refute the man's claims to have kept all of these commandments. He did, however, get straight to the root issue: that to outwardly obey is not sufficient. One must be *willing* to give all we have up to Jesus as an indication that we genuinely want to be His followers, thereby acknowledging Him as both Lord and Master.

Love God and Your Neighbor

> One of the teachers of the law came and heard them debating. Noticing that Jesus had given them a good answer, he asked him, "Of all the commandments, which is the most important?" "The most important one," answered Jesus, "is this: 'Hear, O Israel, the Lord our God, the Lord is one. Love the Lord your God with all your heart and with all your soul and with all your mind and with all your strength.' The second is this: 'Love your neighbor as yourself.' There is no commandment greater than these." (Mark 12:28–31; see also Romans 13:9–12)

It is of great significance that out of the hundreds of directives of scripture, Jesus, Himself, should choose these two to summarize all the rest. God's synopsis of His own commandments is the open display of love—for Him and for each other—as the outworking of our obedience (for commands are designed and given to be obeyed, are they not?).

To Willingly Share the Gospel

> "So I [the Gentile, Cornelius] sent for you immediately, and it was good of you to come. Now we are all here in the presence of God to listen to everything the Lord has commanded you to tell us." Then Peter began to speak: "I now realize how true it is that God does not show favoritism but accepts men from every nation who fear him and do what is right. You know the message God sent to the people of Israel, telling the good news of peace through Jesus Christ, who is Lord of all. (Acts 10:33-36)

> He commanded us to preach to the people and to testify that he is the one whom God appointed as judge of the living and the dead. All the prophets testify about him that *everyone* who believes in him receives forgiveness of sins through his name." (Acts 10:42–43)

This passage marks a pivotal point in the history of Christianity. Here, as in other passages in the book, the realization of the universality of the gospel message is being dealt with. What makes this section critical is that those who have been exclusive in their attitudes about spiritual matters ("We're correct in our theology; too bad rest of you aren't quite there.") were now having to deal with their willingness to present the message of salvation to those who were not like them. To adopt this perspective meant turning their backs on all of the religious traditions that made the Jews, exclusively, God's choice for blessing. This was, no doubt, very difficult for them to deal with, but it was God's command nonetheless.

A Spirit of Repentance

> Therefore since we are God's offspring, we should not think that the divine being is like gold or silver or stone—an image made by man's design and skill. In the past God overlooked such ignorance, but now he commands all people everywhere to repent. For he has set a day when he will judge the world with justice by the man he has appointed. He has given proof of this to all men by raising him from the dead. (Acts 17:29–31)

The warning of judgment is real. It *will* happen. We will all be judged by the holy, almighty, and infallible God. To prepare for this event, we are all called upon to repent: pagans, certainly, but believers as well. We cannot hope to stand before God's judgment apart from the cleansing provided by the blood of the Lamb of God, and our acceptance of that cleansing as sufficient payment for all of our failures and sins. Only through acknowledging Jesus Christ as living LORD can we rely on His mercy and hope to escape His justice. Repentance, therefore, is critical. 2 Corinthians 5:10 tells us that, "We must all appear before the judgment seat of Christ, that each one may receive what is due him for the things done while in the body, whether good or bad."

The Ten Commandments

> And God spoke all these words: I am the LORD your God, who brought you out of Egypt, out of the land of slavery.

> You shall have no other gods before me.

> You shall not make for yourself an idol in the form of anything in heaven above or on the earth beneath or in the waters below. You shall not bow down to them or worship them; for I, the LORD your God, am a jealous God, punishing the children for the sin of the fathers to the third and fourth generation of those who hate me, but showing love to a thousand [generations] of those who love me and keep my commandments.

> You shall not misuse the name of the LORD your God, for the LORD will not hold anyone guiltless who misuses his name.

> Remember the Sabbath day by keeping it holy. Six days you shall labor and do all your work, but the seventh day is a Sabbath to the LORD

your God. On it you shall not do any work, neither you, nor your son or daughter, nor your manservant or maidservant, nor your animals, nor the alien within your gates. For in six days the LORD made the heavens and the earth, the sea, and all that is in them, but he rested on the seventh day. Therefore the LORD blessed the Sabbath day and made it holy.

Honor your father and your mother, so that you may live long in the land the LORD your God is giving you.

You shall not murder.

You shall not commit adultery.

You shall not steal.

You shall not give false testimony against your neighbor.

You shall not covet your neighbor's house. You shall not covet your neighbor's wife, or his manservant or maidservant, his ox or donkey, or anything that belongs to your neighbor. (Exodus 20:1–17)

Even in this original list of God's commandments, we find our attitude to be of central importance. Murder is an act, you say, not an attitude, yet what precipitates murder? According to 1 John 3:15, "Anyone who hates his brother is a murderer." Adultery is likewise an action, yet Christ taught that "anyone who looks at a woman lustfully has already committed adultery with her *in his heart"* (Matthew 5:28). Lying is also an action, but it, too, is brought about by the manifestation of an inner attitude, that of unfaithfulness. Leviticus 6:1–5 outlines this truth for us:

> The LORD said to Moses: "If anyone sins and is *unfaithful to the LORD* by deceiving his neighbor about something entrusted to him or left in his care or stolen, or if he cheats him, or if he finds lost property and lies about it, or if he swears falsely, or if he commits any such sin that people may do—when he thus sins and becomes guilty, he must return what he has stolen or taken by extortion, or what was entrusted to him, or the lost property he found, or whatever it was he swore falsely about. He must make restitution in full, add a fifth of the value to it and give it all to the owner on the day he presents his guilt offering."

Well, the point is established that obedience to God's commands is imperative if we are to validate our faith. Even outsiders are right in judging believers by this standard, according to John 13:35: "All men will know that you are my disciples *if* you love one another."

Be reminded, as well, of John 15:9–17:

> As the Father has loved me, so have I loved you. Now remain in my love. If you obey my commands, you will remain in my love, just as I have obeyed my Father's commands and remain in his love. I have told you this so that my joy may be in you and that your joy may be complete. My *command* is this: *Love each other as I have loved you.* Greater love has no one than this, that he lay down his life for his friends.

You are my friends if you do what I command.
I no longer call you servants, because a servant
does not know his master's business. Instead,
I have called you friends, for everything that
I learned from my Father I have made known
to you. You did not choose me, but I chose
you and appointed you to go and bear fruit—
fruit that will last. Then the Father will give
you whatever you ask in my name. This is my
command: Love each other.

1 Peter 1:13–2:3 further encourages holiness by pointing out
how we've been born again through the living and enduring Word
of God:

Therefore, *prepare your minds for action*; be self-
controlled; set your hope fully on the grace to
be given you when Jesus Christ is revealed. As
obedient children, do not conform to the evil
desires you had when you lived in ignorance.
But just as he who called you is holy, so be holy
in all you do; for it is written: *"Be holy, because I
am holy."* Since you call on a Father who judges
each man's work impartially, live your lives as
strangers here in reverent fear. For you know
that it was not with perishable things such as
silver or gold that you were redeemed from the
empty way of life handed down to you from
your forefathers, but with the precious blood of
Christ, a lamb without blemish or defect. He
was chosen before the creation of the world, but
was revealed in these last times for your sake.
Through him you believe in God, who raised
him from the dead and glorified him, and so

your faith and hope are in God. Now that you have purified yourselves by obeying the truth so that you have sincere love for your brothers, *love one another deeply*, from the heart. For you have been born again, not of perishable seed, but of imperishable, *through the living and enduring word of God.* For, "All men are like grass, and all their glory is like the flowers of the field; the grass withers and the flowers fall, but the word of the Lord stands forever." And this is the word that was preached to you. Therefore, rid yourselves of all malice and all deceit, hypocrisy, envy, and slander of every kind. Like newborn babies, crave pure spiritual milk, so that by it you may grow up in your salvation, now that you have tasted that the Lord is good.

Surely, with all this scripture as encouragement, you and I can turn to God for forgiveness and then turn to Him and others in love. In this way, we can defeat the temptation to be self-centered and focus our lives instead on loving Jesus and those people for whom He died.

Pragmatic Materialism

This worldview is the second most commonly adhered to in the Western world. Slightly more subtle than self-centeredness, this view is nonetheless destructive in its effects. What works here and now, where the bottom line *is* the bottom line? What will it cost? If I think buying into the whole thing costs too much, how much do I really need to get by?

Michael faced this problem in the church member who worked for him, remember? He wanted to be thought of as a good, churchgoing kind of guy but didn't want to miss out on the off-color stories in the shop. You might believe that salvation is important. You may even want the benefits of possessing it. You even sort of wish that you could be 100 percent sold out for God. But perhaps you think you can't pay the price. Why not? That's what we hope to address in the final portion of this chapter.

To begin with, this is not a new problem, but it *is* a biblical problem; at least, scripture directly addresses this dilemma, for our benefit. The bottom line? "What must I do to get ..." Here's the now-familiar story from Matthew 19 and 20, but considered from a different perspective this time. In summary, remember there was the young man who came up to Jesus in verse 16 and asked, "Teacher, what good thing must I do to get eternal life?" After Jesus had answered the young man,

> Peter answered him, "We have left everything to follow you! What then will there be for us?" Jesus said to them, "I tell you the truth, at the renewal of all things, when the Son of Man sits on his glorious throne, you who have followed me will also sit on twelve thrones, judging the twelve tribes of Israel. And everyone who has left houses or brothers or sisters or father or mother or children or fields for my sake will receive a hundred times as much and will inherit eternal life. But many who are first will be last, and many who are last will be first.

> "For the kingdom of heaven is like a landowner who went out early in the morning to hire men to work in his vineyard. He agreed to pay them a denarius for the day and sent them into his vineyard. About the third hour he went out and saw others standing in the marketplace doing nothing. He told them, 'You also go and work

in my vineyard, and I will pay you whatever is right.' So they went. He went out again about the sixth hour and the ninth hour and did the same thing. About the eleventh hour he went out and found still others standing around. He asked them, 'Why have you been standing here all day long doing nothing?' 'Because no one has hired us,' they answered. He said to them, 'You also go and work in my vineyard.' When evening came, the owner of the vineyard said to his foreman, 'Call the workers and pay them their wages, beginning with the last ones hired and going on to the first.' The workers who were hired about the eleventh hour came and each received a denarius. So when those came who were hired first, they expected to receive more. But each one of them also received a denarius. When they received it, they began to grumble against the landowner. 'These men who were hired last worked only one hour,' they said, 'and you have made them equal to us who have borne the burden of the work and the heat of the day.' But he answered one of them, 'Friend, I am not being unfair to you. Didn't you agree to work for a denarius? Take your pay and go. I want to give the man who was hired last the same as I gave you. Don't I have the right to do what I want with my own money? Or are you envious because I am generous?' So the last will be first, and the first will be last."

Now as Jesus was going up to Jerusalem, he took the twelve disciples aside and said to them, "We are going up to Jerusalem, and the Son of Man will be betrayed to the chief priests and the teachers of the law. They will condemn him to death and will turn him over to the Gentiles to be mocked and flogged and crucified. On the third day he will be raised to life!" Then the mother of Zebedee's sons came to Jesus with her sons and, kneeling down, asked a favor of him. "What is it you want?" he asked. She said, "Grant that one of these two sons of mine may sit at your right and the other at your left in your kingdom." "You don't know what you are asking," Jesus said to them. "Can you drink the cup I am going to drink?" "We can," they answered. Jesus said to them, "You will indeed drink from my cup, but to sit at my right or left is not for me to grant. These places belong to those for whom they have been prepared by my Father." When the ten heard about this, they were indignant with the two brothers.

Jesus called them together and said, "You know that the rulers of the Gentiles lord it over them, and their high officials exercise authority over them. Not so with you. Instead, whoever wants to become great among you must be your servant, and whoever wants to be first must be your slave—just as the Son of Man did not come to be served, but to serve, and to give his life as a ransom for many." (Matthew 19:27–20:28)

Did you observe the flow of events in this selection? First, a young ruler asks, "What will it cost?" (But it seems that he was only willing to give just enough to get what he wanted.) Next Peter asks, "What's in it for us?" Then James and John's mother goes to bat for them to find out what *their* reward will be. At this point, the other disciples *all* got riled up (presumably because they also wanted those places of honor).

Finally, Jesus gave His masterful teaching on the nature of honorable leadership: *to have an attitude of willingness.* This willingness was to extend even to the lengths of willingly choosing to become the servant (or even slave) to the others. This was to be the case, even though they may have felt that the others were no more worthy of elevated rank than they were. Once again, my friend, the bottom line, in reality, is attitude. It's ultimately the severe contrast between "What must I give up to get?" and "What may I offer?"

I submit to you that there is no reason to assume that the operational principles of greatness in God's economy have altered one iota from those He told us two millennia ago. How much will it cost? It will cost you your willingness to give over everything to Jesus. How much do you need to get by? It's an all-or-nothing proposition. You can't just about have Him as Lord. It's rather like the concept of being slightly pregnant. Either you are or you aren't. It's the same with Lordship. Either God is the unquestioned Master, the Boss, or He isn't. There simply is no way, logically or biblically, for there to be any other path to follow. As I pointed out in chapter 6, you are either with Him or against Him (Luke 11:23). As Christians, you and I must, *in fact* (not just in word), live with God in charge (James 1:22). This means we cannot be self-centered, self-protecting, or self-fulfilling. We must, in reality, be God-centered, Jesus-serving, and Spirit-honoring. We can no longer operate from our society's common base of materialistic pragmatism. Our confidence and security must be found in the person and work of Jesus Christ alone.

If the goal of a true believer's life is holiness (1 Peter 1:16), then reaching that goal becomes a lifelong pursuit, and that takes discipline and effort. I guess we could liken it to athletes in training. They know the time they need to match in order to qualify and what it takes to reach that time. They won't sit around for several months and then run the day before the event to see if they are ready. No, they actually run every day and track their progress toward their desired end. If our desired end is to be holy, like God, should we expend any less discipline or effort toward our goal?

You see, at its core, Christianity is not pragmatic; it's supernatural. Neither you nor I can begin to live out the simplest foundational concepts of Scripture in our own strength and with our own abilities. I can't love my wife the way Jesus loves the church (Ephesians 5:25). None of us naturally prays without stopping (Ephesians 6:18). We certainly aren't always rejoicing, without His Spirit (Philippians 4:4). And it's fairly obvious that we don't all love God with our whole hearts, nor do we fully love our neighbors as we love and care for ourselves (Luke 10:27).

Clearly, the life of a proper Christian experience is a truly supernatural life, one that is to be lived above the philosophies and "isms" of our humanistic and materialistic society. Our God is fundamentally holy, and we have already been reminded that we are both required and empowered by the Holy Spirit to be the same (1 Peter 1:15–16). And this glorious truth is in complete contrast to any other worldview, belief, system, or religion ever devised by anyone else. (Thanks be to God for His indescribable gifts.) Living completely in His strength—indwelt and empowered by His Holy Spirit—is the *only* way that we are able to actually live out our faith in love.

10

The Basis of Judgment

Is this problem of a lack of biblical spirituality really as severe as I seem to be insisting it is? If it is anywhere close, why haven't we seen it coming and averted its disastrous effects? Will my faith matter here?

IS THE PROBLEM THAT SEVERE?

To address this first question, I've chosen not to use statistics or studies, which can sometimes seem more applicable to other groups than to us; they also become outdated quickly. Instead, I'll address the issue by raising other, pertinent questions and allow you to draw conclusions about your own life. In the final analysis, that's the bona fide concern to most of us anyway: How does this apply to me in my situation? Does this really matter to me?

As we begin, I remind you to go through the chapter with pen and paper in hand. It often helps to jot down a few notes to hang your thoughts on as you address important issues.

First of all, do you feel saved? Now, I know all the good things done by the fact-before-faith teaching, but sometimes, we may throw the baby out with the bath water by dismissing feelings too easily.

(Fact-before-faith affirms that it is of paramount importance to know that your salvation is sure, based on the person and work of Jesus Christ alone, as revealed in Scripture, without any merit on our part, regardless of how you might feel at any point.) But if this were all there were to it, why would Scripture refer so often to things like peace (Colossians 3:15), life to the full (John 10:10), joy (Romans 14:17), and gladness (Acts 2:46) in relation to our salvation? It's reasonable to take these and other words like them at face value, based on the inspiration of Scripture. These terms do not describe facts; they are words that describe how one feels. So do you feel saved? Are you enjoying any of these biblical effects of your salvation? If you aren't, you might need to deal with one of the issues addressed in this book.

Another question that speaks to the seriousness of my proposition: How do you perceive the prayer life, worship, and Christian service (or anything else we've discussed so far) of the people in your congregation (including yourself) in light of what we have studied? Do these areas seem vibrant rather than the cultural norm? If not, could these be indicators of spiritual weakness in your church? I raise questions about the church as a whole simply as a context for addressing the potential weaknesses of each of us, as individual members of it. For we, as individuals within the church, are the primary audience for this entire book.

What are your general observations about the perceived attitudes of most Christians you know? While none of us can really tell what someone else is thinking, we can at least observe their behavior. Do they consistently reflect the true image of the Jesus of the Bible or a more refined, acceptable, and culturally adapted version? Are they completely committed to the Lord? Are they living primarily to His glory? If not, might the problem be spiritual coolness (an issue addressed in this book)? Might they be more concerned with appearing culturally correct rather than being biblically correct? Now, what about yourself? Again, the aim of this book is to help each of us to address our own lives, not those of others.

WHY WEREN'T WE WARNED?

The second question that I raised to open this chapter was, why haven't we seen this coming and tried to avert its disastrous effects? As has been my habit throughout this book, I refer you to God's Word, the Bible, for direction and answers. But before we look at specific scriptures, we need to acknowledge that this is not a new problem, nor is it a rare occurrence; quite the opposite. Throughout time, we humans have had the innate ability to completely miss the point of godly living. From the earliest records of the faithful up to the present, we have struggled with our willingness to relate honestly to God. Our problem today, though, is now too severe to ignore and too devastating in its effects not to address.

Does this quote sound reasonable to you? "If you do what is right, will you not be accepted? But if you do not do what is right, sin is crouching at your door; it desires to have you, but you must master it."

This record of dealing with sin comes from one of the earliest recorded conversations between God and a man. It is found in Genesis 4:7, when the LORD was speaking to Cain just before he killed his brother. Do you grasp the significance of this? Cain had just finished talking to God. He had been warned about the effects of sin. But in the very next verse, he murdered his own brother. He had just been directly warned by God; why didn't he see it coming?

Consider this second example, taken from Matthew 16:21–23. Here, Peter has just been told by Jesus that He must be killed but will rise on the third day. What was Peter's response? Peter rebuked Him by saying, "Never, Lord!" The man has just been told something by Jesus, and Peter turns around and corrects God. Peter was convinced that he knew better than Jesus. Does that approach have just a tiny ring of familiarity to it?

There is also a warning given to a later church, the one in Laodicea, recorded in Revelation 3:15–18:

> I know your deeds, that you are neither cold nor
> hot. I wish you were either one or the other!

> So, because you are lukewarm—neither hot nor cold—I am about to spit you out of my mouth. You say, "I am rich; I have acquired wealth and do not need a thing." But you do not realize that you are wretched, pitiful, poor, blind and naked. I counsel you to buy from me gold refined in the fire, so you can become rich; and white clothes to wear, so you can cover your shameful nakedness; and salve to put on your eyes, so you can see.

This congregation was unable to realize their own situation; it was just as debilitating as the others we have read about. Their judgment was also equally sure, and they were being told it was coming. Jesus was "about to spit [them] out." They were being plainly warned.

Well, so are we, for we have all of these examples and more. Remember how many prophets claimed that the people were doing the right things (offering the right sacrifices, for example), but their hearts were not right before God? They were missing exactly the same things as the scribes and Pharisees were in Jesus's day.

> Woe to you, teachers of the law and Pharisees, you hypocrites! You give a tenth of your spices—mint, dill and cummin. But you have neglected the more important matters of the law—justice, mercy and faithfulness. You should have practiced the latter, without neglecting the former. (Matthew 23:23)

Again, please take note that the most important matters of the law were not what we would say are laws at all. They are justice, mercy, and faithfulness; again, these are attitudes and their resulting actions.

We have looked at a few examples of people who didn't see God's judgment coming, even though they had been alerted. Surely you would agree that we've been adequately warned as well, even if only by their bad examples. So why, then, did they miss out? More importantly, why do we miss it? There are at least two possible explanations.

First, we can't see the obvious. Here are some explanations that tell us why we can't see correctly. According to 2 Corinthians 4:4, "The god of this age has blinded the minds of unbelievers, so that they cannot see the light of the gospel of the glory of Christ, who is the image of God."

While this is written about non-Christians, it points out that one function of Satan is to blind people from a proper view of Christ. Furthermore, we have Jesus's own words: "For false Christs and false prophets will appear and perform great signs and miracles *to deceive even the elect*—if that were possible" (Matthew 24:24).

This pattern of deception will continue to the very end of the age. This is further substantiated by Paul's writings in 2 Corinthians 11, starting at verse 13:

> For such men are false apostles, deceitful workmen, masquerading as apostles of Christ. And no wonder, for Satan himself masquerades as an angel of light. It is not surprising, then, if his servants masquerade as servants of righteousness.

Part of the reason we're not aware of our failure to live as God wishes us to is that we are deceived. We literally do not see that we are falling short of the glory of God's perfection (see also Romans 3:21–26).

Second, we are unaware of the seriousness of our situation because of our own sin. The following verses are but a sampling of many. They could certainly apply to us and our churches, as well as to those they were originally written about. We examined Galatians 3:1–5 earlier in a different context. Look at it again:

> You foolish Galatians! Who has bewitched you? Before your very eyes Jesus Christ was clearly portrayed as crucified. I would like to learn just one thing from you: Did you receive the Spirit by observing the law, or by believing what you heard? Are you so foolish? After beginning with the Spirit, are you now trying to attain your goal by human effort? Have you suffered so much for nothing—if it really was for nothing? Does God give you his Spirit and work miracles among you because you observe the law, or because you believe what you heard?

This question, worded a bit differently, might ask, Are you saved to *perform* like a Christian or to keep *becoming* one? Stop and think about this for a moment. What do you think these verses might be warning you about? Is there anything that may be clouding your faith that is stopping you from expressing it in love? You can confidently let the love of Christ purify, uplift, and equip you to freely live as He wants you to today.

WHAT ABOUT US?

The fundamental basis of judgment is made clear by Christ Himself in John 12:44–50:

> Then Jesus cried out, "Whoever believes in me does not believe in me only, but in the one who sent me. The one who looks at me is seeing the one who sent me. I have come into the world as a

light, so that no one who believes in me should stay in darkness.

If anyone hears my words but does not keep them, I do not judge that person. For I did not come to judge the world, but to save the world. *There is a judge for the one who rejects me and does not accept my words; the very words I have spoken will condemn them at the last day.* For I did not speak on my own, but the Father who sent me commanded me to say all that I have spoken. I know that his command leads to eternal life. So whatever I say is just what the Father has told me to say."

This foundational statement cannot be misunderstood: accepting the work of Jesus Christ is what forms the sole basis of God the Father's judgment. Jesus has come to offer Himself as our Savior and Lord. Our acceptance of Him in that role is what determines our destiny hereafter.

For another insight from God's Word, we move on to Ephesians 4:20–31:

You, however, did not come to know Christ that way. Surely you heard of him and were taught in him in accordance with the truth that is in Jesus. You were taught, with regard to your former way of life, to *put off your old self* which is being corrupted by its deceitful desires; to be made *new in the attitude of your minds;* and to *put on the new self* created to be like God in true *righteousness and holiness.* Therefore each of you must *put off falsehood* and speak truthfully to his neighbor, for we are all members of one body. "In your *anger* do not sin." Do not let the sun go down while you are still angry, and do

not give the devil a foothold. He who has been
stealing must steal no longer, but must work,
doing something useful with his own hands,
that he may have something to share with those
in need. Do not let any *unwholesome talk* come
out of your mouths, but only what is *helpful* for
building others up according to their needs,
that it may benefit those who listen. And *do
not grieve the Holy Spirit of God*, with whom
you were sealed for the day of redemption. Get
rid of all *bitterness, rage and anger, brawling and
slander, along with every form of malice.*

Do you see how often the internal aspects of Christianity are
emphasized and contrasted to the characteristics of our former style
of living? In light of these verses, evaluate for yourself how the
demonstration of your life in Christ Jesus is to be understood:

Be kind and compassionate to one another,
forgiving each other, just as in Christ God
forgave you. Be imitators of God, therefore,
as dearly loved children and live a life of love,
just as Christ loved us and gave himself up for
us as a fragrant offering and sacrifice to God.
(Ephesians 4:32–5:2)

Now, what about the enemies of your soul? What damage can
they do?

Who shall separate us from the love of Christ? Shall
trouble or hardship or persecution or famine or
nakedness or danger or sword? As it is written:
"For your sake we face death all day long; we
are considered as sheep to be slaughtered." No,

in all these things we are more than conquerors through him who loved us. For I am convinced that neither death nor life, neither angels nor demons, neither the present nor the future, nor any powers, neither height nor depth, nor anything else in all creation, will be able to separate us from the love of God that is in Christ Jesus our Lord. (Romans 8:35–39)

The distressing situation is that, while we cannot be separated from the love of Christ, we *can* be separated from fellowship with Him. We can be separated by our sin. Hear what God says through the prophet Isaiah:

Surely the arm of the LORD is not too short to save, nor his ear too dull to hear. But your iniquities have separated you from your God; your sins have hidden his face from you, so that he will not hear. (Isaiah 59:1–2)

Isaiah 29:13–15 reminds us that:

The Lord says: "These people come near to me with their mouth and honor me with their lips, but their hearts are far from me. Their worship of me is made up only of rules taught by men. Therefore once more I will astound these people with wonder upon wonder; the wisdom of the wise will perish, the intelligence of the intelligent will vanish. Woe to those who go to great depths to hide their plans from the LORD, who do their work in darkness and think, 'Who sees us? Who will know?' You turn things upside down,

as if the potter were thought to be like the clay!
Shall what is formed say to him who formed it,
'He did not make me.' Can the pot say of the
potter, 'He knows nothing'?"

These passages, along with the selected verses already referred
to from 1 John and Romans, remind us that it is we who are the
enemies of our own souls. We are often, in fact, our own worst
enemy (short of Satan himself). The problem becomes acute, not
just when we sin, but when we don't admit that we have sinned or
don't repent of it. How much wiser it would be to simply agree with
God's scrutiny of our lives and accept His provision for a victorious
life. Instead, we often persist in our habitual pattern of being "the
blind leading the blind" (Matthew 15:14). If we are not routinely
experiencing the fullness of our salvation, something is probably
wrong. I urge you, by God's grace, seek Him earnestly. Find out
what the problem is (James 1:5–7), then act. Plead for God's mercy
and grace. Trust Him to do all that He wants to do in your life.

For this reason I kneel before the Father, from
whom his whole family in heaven and on
earth derives its name. I pray that out of his
glorious riches he may strengthen you with
power through his Spirit *in your inner being,* so
that Christ may dwell in your hearts through
faith. And I pray that you, being rooted and
established in love, may have power, together
with all the saints, to *grasp* how wide and long
and high and deep is the love of Christ, and
to know this love that surpasses knowledge—
that you may be filled to the measure of all the
fullness of God. Now to him who is able to do
immeasurably more than all we ask or imagine,

> *according to his power that is at work within us,* to him be glory in the church and in Christ Jesus throughout all generations, for ever and ever! Amen. (Ephesians 3:14–21)

Wow.

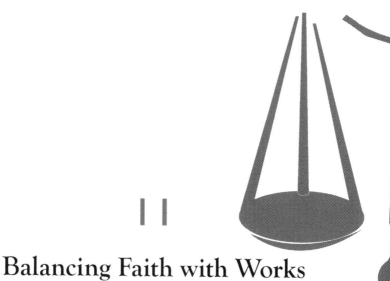

Balancing Faith with Works

The Bible relates beliefs and actions in at least three areas: with God; in relation to salvation; and as it pertains to a believers' lifestyle.

GOD AND JESUS

Humankind has an ongoing infatuation with combining doing and believing; we seem unable to separate the two, but sometimes, we confuse them. This is illustrated very clearly in the questions asked of Jesus, as cited earlier in Chapter 9, in the "What must we do to get?" account from the gospels. The questioners also expected the reverse to be true: that anyone who demanded to be believed had to show that he was worth believing. John 6:30 says, "They asked Jesus, 'What miraculous sign then will you give that we may see it and believe you? What will you do?'"

Jesus gave sound answers to that challenging question of the relationship between belief and works. He said (in John 10:37–38),

> "Do not believe me unless I do what my Father does. But if I do it, even though you do not believe me, believe the miracles, that you may

> know and understand that the Father is in me,
> and I in the Father."

And again in John 14:10:

> "Don't you believe that I am in the Father, and that
> the Father is in me? The words I say to you are
> not just my own. Rather, it is the Father, *living
> in me*, who is doing his work."

The application is clear: Good works flow out of a heart, attitude, spirit, mind-set, or motivation that is controlled by God. God, Himself, has declared that even the good works of our Lord Jesus were done as a result of the servant-relationship that He had with the Father, who was in Him. Because of this demonstration of divine control, Jesus was able to live a life of power and conviction. This controlling presence of the Father was seen by others as well, causing them to respond to Jesus's claims, by faith. They could see His divinity evidenced in His works; in one case, His omniscience (John 16:30):

> Now we can see that you know all things and that
> you do not even need to have anyone ask you
> questions. This makes us believe that you came
> from God.

(Remember, it is still God's work that we are considering in this first section.) Be assured that since Jesus's work was done by faith, so ought ours to be. It follows, then, that Paul is also reasonable in his encouragement to us to seek to know God deeply, in His power, when he writes in Ephesians 1:18–19,

> I pray also that the eyes of your heart may be
> enlightened in order that you may know the

hope to which he has called you, the riches of
his glorious inheritance in the saints, and his
incomparably great power for us who believe.
That power is like the working of his mighty
strength.

Paul also encourages us to be carefully (and not gullibly) involved
in God's work, via his letter to Timothy, which shows once again a
vital connection between belief and action:

> Command certain men not to teach false doctrines
> any longer nor to devote themselves to myths
> and endless genealogies. These promote
> controversies rather than *God's work—which is
> by faith.* (1 Timothy 1:3b–4)

> And we also thank God continually because, when
> you received the word of God, which you heard
> from us, you accepted it not as the word of men,
> but as it actually is, the word of God, which is at
> work in you who believe. (1 Thessalonians 2:13)

What is the conclusion of the relationship between belief and
action, as demonstrated by God, Himself? Is it not that He worked
out His desires through Christ's obedience? This is what we have
seen in the life of Jesus, that He came and fulfilled Scripture by
His very life. Our willingness to fit in to the mold of Scripture is
therefore vital in our knowing how to strike this same balance,
which we so much need in our lives.

SALVATION

This Word that we are to know and obey clearly teaches that
salvation is not a result of our good works. It is a gift of God, freely
given to us by the Holy Spirit, through faith in the teachings of the

Bible about salvation. Yet there is also a clear connection between our salvation and our resultant good deeds.

> For it is by grace you have been saved, through faith—and this not from yourselves, it is the gift of God—not by works, so that no one can boast. For we are God's workmanship, created in Christ Jesus *to do good works*, which God prepared in advance for us to do. (Ephesians 2:8–10)

The whole theme of salvation combines belief and action in balance. First, we must always begin by recognizing that it is God who has provided for our salvation, through Jesus Christ.

> But we ought always to thank God for you, brothers loved by the Lord, because from the beginning God chose you to be saved through the sanctifying work of the Spirit and through belief in the truth. (2 Thessalonians 2:13)

While salvation is clearly God's gift to us, we have an obligation to seek it. If this seeking is genuinely prompted by the Spirit, we will understand that the work we must do to secure salvation is to believe in Jesus as Savior and Lord. In other words, even this work is not work in the usual sense, but believing, or faith. Again, we have the plain and helpful teachings of the Son of God to lead us in understanding how this happens:

> Jesus answered, "I tell you the truth, you are looking for me, not because you saw miraculous signs but because you ate the loaves and had your fill. Do not work for food that spoils, but for food that endures to eternal life, which the Son of

Man will give you. On him God the Father has placed his seal of approval." Then they asked him, "What must we do to do the works God requires?"

Jesus answered, "The work of God is this: to believe in the one he has sent." So they asked him, "What miraculous sign then will you give that we may see it and believe you? What will you do? Our forefathers ate the manna in the desert; as it is written: 'He gave them bread from heaven to eat.'"

Jesus said to them, "I tell you the truth, it is not Moses who has given you the bread from heaven, but it is my Father who gives you the true bread from heaven. For the bread of God is he who comes down from heaven and gives life to the world."

"Sir," they said, "from now on give us this bread." Then Jesus declared, *"I am the bread of life.* He who comes to me will never go hungry, and he who *believes* in me will never be thirsty. But as I told you, you have seen me and still you do not believe. *All that the Father gives me will come to me*, and whoever comes to me I will never drive away. For I have come down from heaven *not to do my will but to do the will of him who sent me."* (John 6:26–39)

Paul clarifies the universal availability of this salvation in Romans 9:30–33:

> What then shall we say? That the Gentiles, who did not pursue righteousness, have obtained it, *a righteousness that is by faith*; but Israel, who pursued a law of righteousness, has not attained it. Why not? Because they pursued it not by faith but as if it were by works. They stumbled over the "stumbling stone." As it is written: "See, I lay in Zion a stone that causes men to stumble, and a rock that makes them fall, and the one who trusts in him will never be put to shame."

Salvation is open to all who, in repentance and faith, believe that Jesus Christ has come to be the Savior of the world by paying the penalty for their sins by dying on the cross, rising from the dead on the third day, and then sending His Spirit to indwell His children. Acts 16:31 affirms, "Believe in the Lord Jesus and you will be saved."

Second, we see that we can only recognize and accept the salvation He has provided for us by appropriating His work, by faith, and that even that faith comes from Him, thereby granting us the ability to believe in His provisional, redemptive work on our behalf. (Ephesians 2:8-9)

In a previous context, we referred to Galatians 3:5–14. Consider it again, in this context:

> Does God give you his Spirit and work miracles among you because you observe the law, or because you believe what you heard? Consider Abraham: "He believed God, and it was credited to him as righteousness." Understand, then, that those who believe are children of Abraham.

The Scripture foresaw that God would justify the Gentiles by faith, and announced the gospel in advance to Abraham: "All nations will be blessed through you." So those who have faith are blessed along with Abraham, the man of faith. All who rely on observing the law are under a curse, for it is written: "Cursed is everyone who does not continue to do *everything* written in the Book of the Law." Clearly no one is justified before God by the law, because, "The righteous will live by faith." The law is not based on faith; on the contrary, "The man who does these things will live by them." Christ redeemed us from the curse of the law by becoming a curse for us, for it is written: "Cursed is everyone who is hung on a tree." He redeemed us in order that the blessing given to Abraham might come to the Gentiles through Christ Jesus, so that by faith we might receive the promise of the Spirit.

Also, consider here the futility of the argument that you can have genuine faith, without that faith showing up in your real, everyday life.

What good is it, my brothers, if a man claims to have faith but has no deeds? Can such faith save him? Suppose a brother or sister is without clothes and daily food. If one of you says to him, "Go, I wish you well; keep warm and well fed" but does nothing about his physical needs, what good is it? In the same way, faith by itself, if it is not accompanied by action, is dead. But someone will say, "You have faith; I have deeds."

Show me your faith without deeds, and I will show you my faith *by* what I do. You believe that there is one God. Good! *Even the demons believe that*—and shudder. You foolish man, do you want evidence that faith without deeds is useless? Was not our ancestor Abraham considered righteous for what he did when he offered his son Isaac on the altar? You see that his faith and his actions were working together, and his faith was made complete by what he did. And the scripture was fulfilled that says, "Abraham believed God, and it was credited to him as righteousness," and he was called God's friend. You see that a person is justified by what he does and not by faith alone. (James 2:14–24)

What does the Scripture say? "Abraham believed God, and it was credited to him as righteousness." Now when a man works, his wages are not credited to him as a gift, but as an obligation. However, to the man who does not work but trusts God who justifies the wicked, his faith is credited as righteousness. David says the same thing when he speaks of the blessedness of the man to whom God credits righteousness apart from works:

"Blessed are they whose transgressions are forgiven, whose sins are covered.

Blessed is the man whose sin the Lord will never count against him."

Is this blessedness only for the circumcised, or also for the uncircumcised? We have been saying that Abraham's faith was credited to him as righteousness. Under what circumstances was it credited? Was it after he was circumcised, or before? It was not after, but before! And he received the sign of circumcision, a seal of the righteousness that he had by faith while he was still uncircumcised. So then, he is the father of all who believe but have not been circumcised, in order that righteousness might be credited to them. And he is also the father of the circumcised who not only are circumcised but who also walk in the footsteps of the faith that our father Abraham had before he was circumcised. (Romans 4:3–12)

This pattern of salvation by faith alone with a result of good works has not changed from ancient times right down to the present. The clear pattern is that those who have been saved will live supernaturally changed lives. Those lives will be characterized by good works.

LIVING AS A BELIEVER

There is a third area where faith and works must combine, and it is only through this combination that our individual Christian lives will be effective. By this point in the book, I trust that it has become clear that we simply cannot be saved by our own acts of goodness. In addition, we have all of the teachings of Scripture, as well as the aid of good Bible-believing churches and teachers to guide us. What creates a problem for us, however, is the life we are to lead after becoming a believer. When should we work? And when should we just believe? What is to be the ongoing relationship between these two facets of our Christian lifestyle?

Scripture seems to guide us in two distinct directions in answer to this question. First, faith is necessary for (and, in fact, leads us into) growth. Second, exercising our faith in obedience to Scripture leads us to do good works. To begin with, then, faith leads us into growth.

> Therefore let us leave the elementary teachings about Christ and go on to maturity, not laying again the foundation of repentance from acts that lead to death, and of faith in God. (Hebrews 6:1)

> Therefore, since we are surrounded by such a great cloud of witnesses, let us throw off everything that hinders *and* the sin that so easily entangles. And let us run with perseverance the race marked out for us, fixing our eyes on Jesus, the pioneer and perfecter of faith. For the joy set before him he endured the cross, scorning its shame, and sat down at the right hand of the throne of God. (Hebrews 12:1–2)

> And so, from the day we heard, we have not ceased to pray for you, asking that you may be filled with the knowledge of his will in all spiritual wisdom and understanding, so as to walk in a manner worthy of the Lord, fully pleasing to him, bearing fruit in every good work and increasing in the knowledge of God. (Colossians 1:9–10)

It is so important for our faith to become strong; our good works must flow out of our faith. It seems reasonable to conclude that a weak faith will result in little significant spiritual work. A strong and vibrant faith will more likely result in increased spiritual value coming out of our efforts. Isn't this what we should all want, that what we do might have significant spiritual value and count for God, that we should faithfully apply what we are becoming? One other thing to consider: if people don't have good works, do they even *have* faith at all? (See James 2.)

Here are some final passages, selected to show us how to let our faith lead us to do things that will have an impact on our world for holiness:

> With this in mind, we constantly pray for you, that our God may count you worthy of his calling, and *that by his power he may fulfill every good purpose of yours and every act* prompted by your faith. (2 Thessalonians 1:11)

> I pray that you may be active in sharing your faith, so that you will have a full understanding of every good thing we have in Christ. (Philemon 1:6)

> Neither do we go beyond our limits by boasting of work done by others. Our hope is that, as your faith continues to grow, our area of activity among you will greatly expand. (2 Corinthians 10:15)

> Not that we lord it over your faith, but we work with you for your joy, because it is by faith you stand firm. (2 Corinthians 1:24)

Finally, Paul gives us this goal to aim for (an epitaph, if you like), which could be the desire for all sincere believers as we come to the end of our lives here on earth:

We continually remember before our God and
Father your work produced by *faith*, your
labor prompted by *love*, and your endurance
inspired by *hope in our Lord Jesus Christ*. (1
Thessalonians 1:3)

So what is your conclusion at this point? Knowing what you
know after reading this book, are you willing to give all you can be
to God? My own conclusion has to be that I must apply all I know
to every routine of life. I know He loves me and wants my love to be
shown by my obedience. I also know that the only thing that counts
is faith expressing itself through love. There is no second alternative,
no higher calling, than to give my life for His holy purposes.

Ephesians 3:16-21 is the best summary of biblical spirituality
that I can leave you with:

I pray that out of his glorious riches he may
strengthen you with power through his Spirit
in your *inner being*, so that Christ may dwell
in your *hearts* through faith. And I pray that
you, being rooted and established in love, may
have power, together with all the saints, to
grasp how wide and long and high and deep is
the love of Christ, and to know this love that
surpasses knowledge—that you may be filled to
the measure of all the fullness of God. Now to
him who is able to do immeasurably more than
all we ask or imagine, according to his power
that is at work within us, to him be glory in
the church and in Christ Jesus throughout all
generations, for ever and ever! Amen.

So let's agree to get on with it. Fill your mind and heart with
His Word. Be fully empowered by His indwelling Holy Spirit. Live

that rich life of faith, poured out in the loving good works that God both commands and empowers you to do, that have been tailored specifically for you. Be completely filled with Him, to His glory and your own sheer delight. God will bless you as you do, and the world around you will be richly blessed by Him, through you.

NOTES

NOTES

NOTES

NOTES

Printed in the United States
By Bookmasters